CLUCK OINK BAA MOO

CLUCK OINK BAA MOO

How to choose, prepare and cook meat and poultry

MIRANDA BALLARD

PHOTOGRAPHY BY STEVE PAINTER

RYLAND PETERS & SMALL

LONDON • NEW YORK

DEDICATION
To my parents, Edward and Jude.

DESIGN, PROP STYLING & PHOTOGRAPHY
 Steve Painter
EDITOR Kate Reeves-Brown
PRODUCTION MANAGER Gordana Simakovic
ART DIRECTOR Leslie Harrington
EDITORIAL DIRECTOR Julia Charles
PUBLISHER Cindy Richards

FOOD STYLIST Lucy McKelvie
US CONTRIBUTING EDITOR Toponia Miller
INDEXER Vanessa Bird

First published in 2015 as *The Modern Meat
Kitchen*. This revised edition published in 2021
by Ryland Peters & Small
20–21 Jockey's Fields
London WC1R 4BW
and
341 E 116th St
New York NY 10029

www.rylandpeters.com

10 9 8 7 6 5 4 3 2 1

ISBN: 978-1-78879-353-7

A CIP record for this book is available from
the British Library.
US Library of Congress CIP data has been
applied for.

RECIPE NOTES

• Both metric and imperial/US cups are included.
Work with one set of measurements and do not
alternate between the two within a recipe.
All spoon measurements given are level:
1 teaspoon/tsp = 5 ml; 1 tablespoon/tbsp = 15 ml.
• Eggs are medium (UK) or large (US), unless
otherwise specified. Uncooked or partially cooked
eggs should not be served to the very old, frail,
young children, pregnant women or those with
compromised immune systems.
• Ovens should be preheated to the specified
temperatures. We recommend using an oven
thermometer. If using a fan-assisted oven, adjust
temperatures according to the manufacturer's
instructions.

FOOD SAFETY

• Cover all meats and store them in a refrigerator.
• Use the freshest meats possible for home-curing.
• Keep raw meat and poultry, and their juices,
away from other foods. After cutting raw meats,
wash cutting boards, utensils and countertops with
hot, soapy water. Cutting boards, utensils and
countertops can be sanitized by using a solution
of 1 tbsp of unscented, liquid chlorine bleach in
4.5 litres/1 gallon of water.
• Uncooked or partially cooked meats should not
be served to the very old, frail, young children,
pregnant women or those with compromised
immune systems.

DISCLAIMER

The information in this book is based on the
author's experience. Guidelines for safety are
given within the recipes and should be followed.
Neither the author nor the publisher can be held
responsible for any harm or injury that arises from
the application of the ideas in this book.

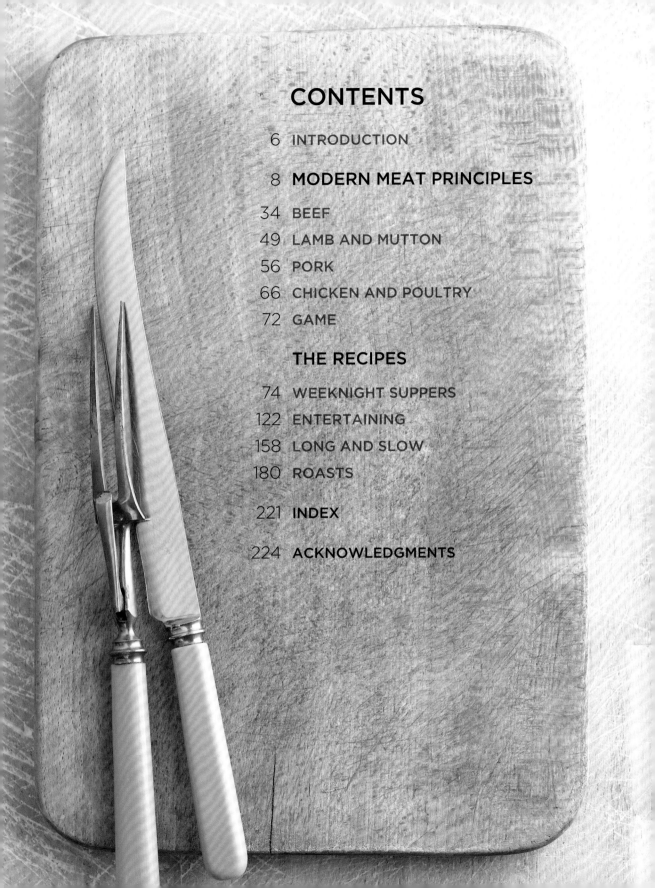

CONTENTS

INTRODUCTION

Writing this book was an absolute treat for me. I have owned a meat company; I am a lover of great farming; I'm a meat eater; I'm an enthusiastic cook; I don't have an unlimited budget for food shopping; and I always seem to be really (really) busy! So I am perfectly placed to put together a great collection of recipes that work within the demands of a modern family lifestyle (mine included).

Of course the recipes in my book (and every other meat recipe ever written) actually start with the farming: the life and origin of the meat and our relationship with it. We don't have to spend a lot of time making a recipe, but we do have an obligation to understand the origins of our meat, and you can do this simply by asking questions of the person selling it to you. In this book I exclusively endorse well-farmed meat, both for the ethics of animal husbandry and for the eating experience. I do this confidently due to the work that I had the pleasure of doing with some of the UK's finest farmers during my time working as a meat retailer.

I also feel confident proposing that a modern meat cook does not need to be detached from the handling of meat. Some recipes here use cuts of meat that I show you how to butcher yourself from larger pieces of meat. I've been delighted to discover a demand for simple home butchery, or 'cooktchery' as I like to call it: the simple cutting of meat at home for cooking, rather than for retail presentation or commercial efficiency. This is exciting, really satisfying and surprisingly easy to do.

I also mention my own limited budget, because as a consumer and a former business owner, I'm not naive about the difficult balance between ethical ideals and a realistic commercial viability. However I do believe I can prove that there is a balance; there is a point where the contract of animal husbandry works and we can still afford it. You'll see that nearly all my recipes have value in mind, from how to utilize a more affordable cut to how to buy a larger piece of meat, which is cheaper per kg/lb., and portion it yourself by freezing batches and chilling leftovers for other recipes.

The average cooking time for the evening meal in the UK has reduced from 55 minutes in the 1970s to just 18 minutes today. Of 2,000 people asked at 4 pm, 1,500 hadn't yet planned what they were going to have for dinner that night. This isn't necessarily a bad thing – we have to embrace these significant changes in our lifestyles and routines, and meat recipes can be some of the easiest, quickest and most nutritious you can choose. Even the recipes with longer cooking times, such as large roasts and braises, are designed with leftovers for later in the week in mind.

This book is about how to get the absolute best and most out of every cut of meat you buy and every recipe you choose to make in your own kitchen at home.

MODERN MEAT PRINCIPLES

Meat has been a fundamental part of our ancestral history and human evolution. Now, in modern society, our relationship with meat has completely evolved too. Though it is still absolutely intrinsic to our lives, we no longer actually need to eat it to survive.

So, here we are, in a new era of meat consumption, a modern collaboration with farming and a modern definition of animal husbandry. Although there are failings, there is also sincerity, commitment and a celebration of good flavour.

The most positive thing that those in the meat industry can do is ask you, the consumer, what you want to know. More than that, they should see if they can help you find the questions you want to ask in the first place. We should never make you feel that, just because you eat meat, you should understand how, for example, it gets to you, why it was priced as it is, how it was farmed, and so on. I'm typing these words on a computer, but I don't understand how the processor is working, nor how it just auto-saved to a 'cloud' thing, and I would be offended if an IT expert made me feel stupid for asking. So, transparency in the meat industry and a true willingness by suppliers to have an open conversation about our meat will empower you with enough knowledge to make the right choices.

So I'm going start this book with by asking four questions – the four questions most often asked by consumers in butchers shops. I hope that one or more of them will appeal to your priorities, too.

1 How do I tell the difference between 'good' meat and 'cheap' meat?
2 What price should I be paying?
3 Where is the meat from?
4 What do I do with it?

These are the four questions you should ask your butcher and feel confident about asking them. To give you a bit of a head start, I'm going to start with the first one – I think it's the most important question for me to try to answer before we begin a collection of recipes that very confidently advocates the use of good meat. On the following pages, we will take a look at the differences between the production of 'cheap' meat and 'good' meat.

Now this is a rather coarse approach to defining farming practices and I don't mean to ignore the complexities and subjectivity of farming, nor do I suggest there isn't a middle ground between these extremes. However I intend for this to be a general case study to compare a chronology of the two ends of the market. I haven't simplified this because I think you need it this way and I do this because it is how I first came to learn about farming myself. It's how I started to become more confident to ask the questions I needed to ask to be able to find where the balance lay between commercial viability and ethics in our former meat business.

I've chosen beef because I come from a beef farming background and I've worked with beef more than any other meat in the last seven years, but the chart is similar for other commercially farmed animals and, indeed, for the breeding of dairy cattle, too. So, on pages 10–11 we start right from the beginning, at conception, and trace the meat through to the retailer.

TASTE

The taste of meat is a fascinating study because it is entirely due to our ancestral history that a sequence of sensory reactions occur at the sight, smell and taste of meat. If you flip the idea from 'I eat this because it's tasty' to 'This is tasty because I eat it and because our ancestors ate it', it gets really interesting.

The ultimate fuel
Like all living things, we need fuel. We ingest food and convert it to fuel. About 2 million years ago, at the *Homo erectus* stage in our evolution, our bodies became bipeds. We were moving, we were evolving, we were making tools, we were hunting and we were eating meat. There is even evidence that we were starting to cook, too.

The energy from the calories in meat did wonders for us – we could hunt, gather, fight and flee better than we ever could before, and we had the strength to survive adverse weather, harsh climates, attacks and other threats to our continued evolution. And as we converted this new fuel, we also absorbed the protein in it, which made our muscles stronger and bigger, and our brains grow and advance. We started to develop social skills, very early communication and a sense of self.

Irresistible taste
Meat is fundamental to our history and we are still hardwired, instinctively, to recognize foods with high fats, sugars, proteins and salts as fuel and, significantly, 'fast fuel'. We love vitamins, minerals and the things that make us feel healthy and alert, but our most basic animal instinct is to survive and if there's something that will make the muscles in our bodies stronger, then we're going to crave it. Indeed, this is why cured meat is often described as 'tasty' and 'flavourful' when our body actually senses 'usable' and 'valuable'.

One of the most common confessions of vegetarians is a yearning for bacon when it is being cooked near them. This is no coincidence at all: the smell triggers the alerts in our heads for salts, fats and proteins mixed together, a super-fuel signal to our caveman ancestors and to us now, too. The tricky part is that we're still tuned to follow this thirst for fats and proteins when we no longer live in a world where we need to run from a wild animal or kill with handheld tools. Today, we think we have control over whether a food tastes good to us, but it's still the food that dictates to us whether we want to eat it – our body's response to a food is what manifests as 'tasty' and our instincts haven't caught up with modern life yet.

Meat in modern diets
One could argue that we don't need meat at all these days, as it has done its job of getting us this far. Though we're not fighting and fleeing so much any more, without the nutritional content of 'good' meat our bodies still lack strength and ability. We must have a well-designed, careful diet of substitutes, inspired by the effects of meat on our bodies, to survive. We have the luxury of the kind of global food chain and food technology that our ancestors – even recent ancestors – could have never imagined, so we can easily choose to follow a vegetarian diet. A lot of how we look and behave and a lot of what we're capable of doing is thanks to eating meat, and good meat is vital to our modern meat-eating diet. I can't stress enough that the difference between 'good' meat and 'cheap' meat is everything. I'll try to explain why over the following pages.

'GOOD' MEAT VERSUS 'CHEAP' MEAT

So let's tackle the question – how do we tell the difference between 'good' meat and 'cheap' meat? And why should we care? Well, we should care for two simple reasons: taste and principles.

'GOOD' MEAT	'CHEAP' MEAT
The pedigree and/or registered bull is rotated through the herd to impregnate the cows.	The cows are artificially inseminated with a stock semen developed from a number of breeds for optimum growth and weight.
The pregnant cow is outdoors (except during extreme temperatures) for the 9-month gestation and fed pasture food: grass, silage, barley, peas.	The pregnant cow is kept indoors, with the rest of the herd, and fed a mixture of pasture, grain, soya, genetically modified (GM) feed, cereals and antibiotics.
The cow will come indoors for labour and be monitored. The calf is born with any assistance necessary. Cow and calf stay indoors for a day or two before returning to the field together.	The cows are scheduled for assisted birthing. The calf may stay for colostrum (first milk) but will be removed from the mother's stall soon after birth to begin its own developed feeding regime of formula milk.
The calf weans for six to eight months, as it naturally moves from the teat to eating grass. A bull calf may be castrated to make a 'steer' for beef, or be assigned for bull breeding in the herd. A female will be assigned to beef or breeding.	The calf has been growing away from the mother the whole time and the mother is being prepared for another insemination or for slaughter.
If assigned to beef, the cow continues to feed itself grass and silage. Some beetroot/beets in the winter, too, perhaps.	The cow is fed growth hormones and high-fat cereals and grain for optimum growth, weight and fats (marbling) in the meat.
The cow might be moved (in a minimum of pairs) from a breeding farm to a finishing farm, depending on the size of the farms involved.	The cow may be moved from a breeding lot to a finishing/feed lot (both indoors). A foreign born calf may be moved to the UK for rearing and finishing.
The cow is scheduled for slaughter between the age of 24 and 30 months old, at an average weight of 400 kg/900 lbs.	The cow is scheduled for slaughter from 18 months old, as soon as it reaches target weight. It may be moved to a third farm for fattening/finishing.
The cow is taken (in a pair to avoid stress and the release of adrenalin) to the slaughterhouse, often the day before, to settle in 'layerage' overnight to calm.	The cow is packed into a cattle lorry/truck with the other cows and taken to the slaughterhouse for immediate slaughter.

'GOOD' MEAT	'CHEAP' MEAT
The cow walks between two high, winding walls – cattle and sheep will inquisitively walk around a corner and this means the cow walks to slaughter without being handled.	The cow is packed into the slaughter space along with the other cows. They are then taken one at a time to the crush and bolt gun.
The soundproof wall goes up. The cow takes its place on the slaughter platform. The soundproof wall goes down. The head is raised up by a slow mechanical arm and the bolt gun moves to the precision-programmed location on the front of the head. The bolt completely implodes the brain. There is no consciousness or brain activity. There is minimized stress for the animal, preventing the release of adrenalin, which toughens the meat.	The wall goes up. The cattle is crushed to be held in position. There are humans around, so the animal is aware of danger and may instinctively release the stress hormone, adrenalin, into the blood (this strengthens the muscles in order to run away). The precision-programmed bolt gun is moved into place and the brain is completely imploded. There is no consciousness or brain activity.
The animal is strung by a rear ankle and the neck is sliced to drain all the blood. The stomach and all fecal matter is drawn. The capacity and pace per bolt-gun line per day is approximately 250 cattle.	The animal is strung by a rear ankle and the neck is sliced to drain all the blood. The capacity and pace per bolt-gun line per day is a minimum of 400 cattle.
An independent vet adjudicates the process, grades the animal and authorizes the traceability tag to be attached to both halves of the carcass, which has been split and the spinal cord removed – the main risk of bovine spongiform encephalopathy (BSE or 'mad cow disease') and Creutzfeldt-Jakob disease (CJD) contamination to the meat.	
The carcass is skinned, offal removed and the body moved to a refrigerator to cool.	The carcass is skinned, offal and stomachs removed, and the body moved to a refrigerator to cool.
The meat is butchered: each traceability marking kept with each quarter; offal trimmed for pet and human food; fats rendered for oils; bones used for marrow and stock; collagen, bone, hooves, hide, etc., removed for by-products ('fifth quarter' refers to the utilization of the entire animal).	The meat is butchered: all commercial meat and products are removed; anything else is refuse. Often intensive slaughterhouses do not have the budget for long-term investment in low-margin by-products and 'fifth quarter'. Sometimes these parts will be shipped for outsourced handling.
The meat is butchered for wholesale or retail. It is marked with the slaughterhouse's hygiene and traceability code and any accreditations and certifications. Prime cuts may be dry-aged or matured in a humidity-controlled refrigerator.	The meat is (often mechanically) butchered, processed for wholesale or retail and coded with the legal requirements. Prime cuts may be wet-aged in vac-pack bags. Small pieces of meat are mechanically separated from the carcass, minced and processed (often called 'pink slime').
It is sold packaged to the consumer through reputable retailers (including supermarkets).	It is packaged and sold to the consumer through national retailers (in particular supermarkets).

PRINCIPLES

So, to the principles of 'good' meat and their origin. If our history is where I argue taste comes from, where and when was the source of our principles? And what do they look like in a modern world?

I have a dream that we could reclassify the term 'meat'. Like how an Aston Martin is a 'car', and a Fiat is a 'car'... but they are not compared as 'cars', in neither price nor product. In fact, you would laugh if a Fiat was suggested as a direct alternative for less money. So when you look down the comparable chronologies in farming practice on pages 10–11, the end product should not equally be called 'meat' because we can prove that the products have been produced in very different ways. That in the same way that one can measure the engineering, design, metalwork, performance, and so on of an Aston Martin, so too can you define and value the end product from the good farming chronology. And, incidentally, the 'cheap' meat column is still the regulated lower end of the market: it does not come near to the criminal activity that occurs in the meat industry.

Maybe the word 'cheap' is too flippant and ambiguous, but could we call the two grades, 'good' meat and 'fast' meat perhaps? That doesn't seem unfair or misleading, as the process to produce cheaper meat is much faster. Then if someone says they are totally happy with 'fast' meat, its flavour and its processes, then that is fine – we accept that they have made an informed decision and are totally aware that they're buying a different product.

I realize, at the same time, that this is the real world and we cannot start a campaign with the scale of meat retail. But just think what a difference it makes, every time a customer asks, 'Excuse me, is this "good" meat?' it sends a ripple through the meat industry, all the way to the farm, and one more animal is reared a little better. That we can individually have such an effect on something as unimaginably immense as the global meat industry is what I love the most – these measurable effects and our fantastically exciting role in supply and demand.

So why are there principles in the first place and what are they? Christien Meindertsma completed an incredible three-year study called 'Pig 05049', in which she tracked the journey of one pig and its by-products to 184 counts of different uses from one pig's body, so unbelievably far beyond pork chops and sausages. She followed the parts to their use in concrete, bread manufacturing, paint, pharmaceuticals, military armament and it is wonderful and fascinating – I recommend the book or 'How Pig Parts Make The World Turn' (2010) introduction on TED online.

And this is where I also have some fun when talking to vegans and vegetarians. To define our principles, one first has to accept the role that meat plays in our modern world, beyond the steak on our plate and the recipes in this book.

The principles of veganism
I would go so far as to say that one can never cut animal products out of one's life completely. I should say that I love debating this point with vegans; I do so with respect and a cheeky smile, because I admire anyone making a positive and rational commitment to their beliefs. That said, here are some things to consider before deciding to go vegan:

1 Evolution, as we've already covered, is where meat had a massive impact on what we look like and are capable of doing today.

2 Good vegetables, which are fertilized by livestock waste, would need science and pesticides to grow without it. If we all stopped eating meat, there would be no meat farms. In the short term, the animals would all be killed

and burnt, and in the long term, there would be no organic or natural fertilizer for the farming and production of crops.

3 Arable farming in general, ploughing/plowing a field of crop kills far more living beings than even a mass intensive livestock farm could kill in a year. It's just that they're little insects, ground-feeding birds and rodents... and it's harder to imagine that they have feelings.

4 Soil is made up of carbon from millions and millions of years of the corroded bodies of these small animals and every size animal.

5 Indeed, it is compressed carbon that is fueling our electricity, our houses, our cars...

6 Meat by-products are used in all kinds of manufacturing and production. There is no meat in your can of green beans, but the production of the mould to make the aluminium can they come in will have likely used pig by-product to make the shape.

7 Of course, there's leather, gelatine in cakes, etc. – the consumer items that are easier to avoid as a vegan, which more directly relate to the animal as we can picture them – but there are animal by-products in soap, toothpaste, shampoo and medicine.

I'm not just trying to antagonize; I mean it from a good place and I'm still very early on in my own journey to understand meat and our relationship with animals. But I feel strongly that to study veganism, vegetarianism and our principles, we must stop looking at meat only in the context of eating meat. For example, there are many uses of animal products, such as the commercial bread raising-agent that includes an ingredient from pig hair. We can live without meat products, we can buy bread that isn't mass produced, we can buy sweets that don't contain gelatine... it's just that our relationship with living beings, and indeed their relationship with each other, goes far beyond purely the rearing and slaughter of livestock. We are blessed with the mental capacity to challenge and question

this larger context where we're a significantly smaller aspect of the symbiosis of all living things, and we should absolutely do that. This earth, this ecology and this biology existed before we were able to question it and so we shouldn't dismiss the wider picture and its limitless impact on our lives and evolution. Examine, challenge... have the conversations.

Once again, it comes back to the practice of 'good' meat versus 'fast' meat, and on the journey of trying to imagine the bigger picture, I become ever more confident to denounce 'fast' meat, as the practices can in no way be described as 'natural'. For example, the process of force-feeding geese to produce foie gras from their liver is not 'natural'. Eating a goose – if we compare our practices to wild carnivores – is 'natural'. Hounds killing a fox is 'natural'; they will do this without human training and assistance; but humans following on a horse and not eating the fox at the end isn't necessarily 'natural'. Maybe the discipline, 'WWWAD?', could be introduced: What Would Wild Animals Do? It's not as simple as this, I do understand that, but to question a few smaller parts of an impossibly large overall question, can surely do no harm. The chronology for 'fast' meat on page 10 is an achievement for modern science but it is so different to our own history and to any other carnivorous animal today. It has gone so far.

If a vegan tells me they would still choose for the animal never to be born, I'm listening. If they say that to die to be eaten is not worth the life they have before slaughter, even if it is the life that the animal would lead if there were no farmers, no human intervention and absolutely no conscious awareness of the lead-up to nor moment of slaughter, I'm listening. I'll obviously ask them how we will redesign not just agriculture but our society, economy and human survival, but I am listening. Vegetarians who are vegetarian for reasons relating to animal welfare, on the other hand, have it all upside down.

I'D RATHER BE A BEEF COW

In the chronology of 'good' meat versus 'cheap' meat on pages 10–11, there was a period of up to 30 months when the animal (either bred outdoors or indoors) is largely left alone to, on a good farm, eat what they want to eat and do what they want to do. If we do a quick chronology for that section for the life for a dairy cow, it offers another view of the role of meat beyond steaks and burgers.

It may surprise you to learn that dairy cows are slaughtered, too. They cannot stay on a farm to die a natural death; it just doesn't happen. To consume dairy without taking responsibility for the end of the life of that dairy-producing animal is irresponsible and infinitely more detached from its life than eating meat.

I would choose not to eat dairy if I were to make a stand against the treatment of animals, and I would certainly choose to be a beef cow over a dairy cow.

Again, I'm not trying to be antagonistic about this, but it's part of the wider argument about animal husbandry, to find a meat and dairy supply that we trust.

Below you'll find a table detailing the differences between what I consider to be 'good' dairies versus 'cheap' dairies.

'GOOD' DAIRY (EXTENSIVE FARMING)	'CHEAP' DAIRY (INTENSIVE FARMING)
The calf is born. If it's a female it will stay with the mother for a few weeks. If the breed, or cross-breed, has a market demand for its beef as well as milk, a bull calf may stay with its mother for milk-fed and/or rosé veal for a few weeks. Usually, though, the bull calf is killed straight away as it will never produce milk for the dairy farm.	The calf is born. If it's a pure dairy herd, the bull calf is killed immediately. If there is a market for the beef, it is taken from the mother after the first day, reared on formula, castrated to become a steer and slaughtered for beef. A female calf may stay with the mother for a short time, but the milk from the mother is the product, so the calf is kept indoors and fed formula.
After weaning, the female calf is fed formula until she becomes a dairy cow and twice a day, she will be herded into the milking parlour, have the pumps attached to her udders and be milked. She will then be herded back to the field.	The female cow becomes a dairy cow. She is kept indoors all day, the pumps are attached to her udders twice a day and she is milked.
The cow may be used for breeding. The most common challenge is mastitis, when the teat ducts contract a bacterial infection, either from the pump (cleanliness and hygiene), the water, or another aspect of the milking parlour.	
The udders need to be 'dipped' to fend off infection. Infection needs to be treated with antibiotics.	
The cow is either slaughtered for beef if it's within the legal killing age or slaughtered for by-products once it stops producing milk or can't be used for breeding.	

WHAT ABOUT PRICE?

It's weird that we buy meat from big national chains of supermarkets. We don't have to comprehend how the system works, but we should try to picture it.

Picture the nearest supermarket to your home, and then picture the meat counter: the ground meat, sausages, burgers, steaks, roasting joints, chicken, ham, bacon, ready-to-eat meals, salamis... Then picture the lorry/truck coming to the back of the store every day to restock the aisle. Now picture the next nearest 10 stores all having a delivery of their own. Then imagine the next 100 nearest, then the next 1,000... and, for the UK, about 5,500 stores of the six main national supermarket chains. In America, over 14,500 supermarket outlets for just the national chains. Then there are regional companies, convenience stores, online retailers, wholesalers and so on. Walmart and Tesco, for example, own more than 3,000 stores each – 3,000 of those meat sections running simultaneously, the whole time, all across the country, with fresh meat.

I don't find it as strange to imagine pallets of ketchup or, for example, breakfast cereals or toilet paper or long-life/shelf-stable products. But meat? How many cows, pigs, lambs, chickens? Fish, how many fish? And all the dairy: milk, cheese, yogurt, ice cream, butter...? The scale is unbelievable.

This brings us to the question of price, by far the biggest factor in our modern meat industry and our modern lives. If meat is considered too expensive, shoppers won't buy it, there will be no profit and the company will go bust. If the meat is priced too cheaply, there may be no money left after the farm, slaughterhouse, chilled delivery company, butchers, electricity and water bills have been paid, as well as the ingredients, packaging, regulations, etc. So there has to be a price point where it can be produced in budget and people will buy it.

And what is 'too expensive'? Factors like income, geography and economy all have to be taken into account but, simply put, if a shopper wants it, they will pay for it. Or maybe the better way to phrase it is: if the customer doesn't want it, they simply won't pay for it.

Be confident asking about pricing – why is one pack of chicken breasts so much cheaper than another? Be polite (it's a sensitive subject), but you should feel comfortable asking a retailer about price.

Mass production

Going back to the thousands upon thousands of meat aisles, the competitive price 'wars' have brought the average price of meat right down, so much so that a lot of our meat in the UK, as well as in the USA, costs less than it did in the 1970s, despite inflation and above-inflation increases in costs of production and transport (such as fuel). This is because:

1 The quality of farming, production, slaughter, butchery, processing, packaging, retailing, etc. has had to come down.

2 The scale of production (to supply those 3,000 stores owned by one company) has had to go up to produce efficiencies.

Put simply, and I know I'm telling you what you already know, the cost of making two beef burgers isn't double the cost to make one; you already had to put the meat through the grinder and weigh out the ingredients and pack it – it's not double the work for the second burger since you were already making one. Similarly, the lorry/truck going to the back of one of the stores was going there anyway, another pack of burgers doesn't double the cost of the fuel. Mass production means the cost of every unit comes down, which is fantastic and where I am least anti-supermarket because they can achieve, through taking on huge risks and liabilities, the economies of scale that small companies can't achieve. These savings are passed onto customers who undoubtedly benefit.

Mass production versus premium quality

Is large-scale mass production really a good thing in meat, given that we haven't yet worked out a way to farm 'good' meat any faster than we do? Or have we found a secret formula to find the balance between the quality of farming and the commercial viability and sustainability of the product any cheaper?

My question to the meat industry is: if we accept mass, how can we make mass better? If supermarket meat cost 10 per cent more, would it be so bad if we bought and ate 10 per cent less? Especially if 10 per cent more on the price meant it was 10 per cent better tasting and better farmed? I know it's not as simple as this, but I'm not going to stop thinking of pricing and principles in simplified questions like this. I'll also accept just as much that if I find something 'too expensive' then maybe I just don't want or need it right now. 'Too expensive' is often used in the place of 'it's just not something I'm looking for at the moment'. If you don't want something then the price will always be expensive. To you.

The economist Richard Thaler used the term 'mental accounting' to describe the sequence of valuations that happens separately in each of our minds when we process the cost of a transaction within the context of the things on which we spend our money, i.e. our priorities, our interests, our restraints, and so on. Things can be expensive to some people and very good value to others. Each customer does some quick mental accounting of their values whilst they decide whether to buy specific products or not.

The average family's grocery bill has dropped 5 per cent in the last 10 years, which may not seem like much, but the significance is that there are still the same number of items in the average shopping trolley/cart. The same groceries just cost 5 per cent less. For this to be the case, all the suppliers of those groceries need to either reduce their prices or reduce the cost of making their product. The majority of meat companies and retailers I've been in the fortunate position to be able to meet are not crooks, they do not think that the consumer is stupid and they are not making enormous profits by exploiting the unquantifiable, unregulated price of your food products. In chilled food, particularly, with the very high additional costs of something as simple as refrigerated storage and transport, the margins are very small. For the 'good guys', taking 5 per cent off their price just isn't realistic for the survival of the company; it has to come out of the product and, for meat, it always comes back to where and how it was farmed.

Very often with meat, it is what falls in and out of favour. I'm at peace with media coverage of meat, even the sensationalized coverage. It exists, it taints and it can mislead, but it generally only targets or appeals to those who probably wouldn't go and ask questions anyway, nor would they welcome the chance to have a conversation with those in the meat industry about meat and farming. 'Good' meat just isn't important to everyone. I'm not being a defeatist, I just always preferred to do a really, really good job for those to whom it is important. In the long term, the positive movement of these people, who have access to good meat and the ripples they make through a national, even global, meat industry is more powerful than I could ever be by howling at the moon about how we need a revolution. Little changes and little improvements to the system will be what regains the grace and respectability of our meat industry. So to our next question...

WHERE IS MY MEAT FROM?

This is a great question to encapsulate all the major factors of farming and producing meat. Don't ever feel like you need to understand the whole process of producing meat. You are responsible for the meat that you purchase and for finding a source that suits your principles, tastes and budget.

There are three important points here: traceability, practice and accountability.

There are a lot of national certifications and accreditations for meat in different countries. I admire them as they are founded on a base of honest beliefs and integrity. They are brilliant at defining where lines can be drawn in practices and helping to communicate these to a consumer who may have very little time (or interest) to carry out the studies themselves. However, they are also brilliant at allowing a consumer to believe that they are the 'right way' and that foods without these accreditations are inferior. They are, however, just accreditations; they're still an optional subscription for the farm to undertake and a cost for them to absorb.

Let's take the 'Organic' certificate (Soil Association in the UK, AOM in Australia, the NOP in conjunction with the USDA in America, ECOCERT in Europe, and so on...). We are better for these regulating bodies, undeniably so. They filter and define practices and have a symbol that is easily recognisable. They reassure you that meat production follows certain principles without you needing to understand the details.

However, I believe they stifle the questions that I'm so desperate for the industry to be asked and answer. They go too far to market meat and stop us from just asking one of the four simple questions I'm trying to answer now. I don't think that's as positive as the initial objective started out to be because all farms are not owned by one organisation and certainly I have never been to even two farms that practise

farming the same way. Carrots, for example, are more easily defined – organic vegetables and arable farming are far from an easy science and rely on massive amounts of skill and experience (and instinct), but the same acreage that can produce 10 tonnes of carrots will produce perhaps 40 beef cattle a year. That's 40 different animals, with different genetics, health and feeding needs, unknowns and variables. Classifying and certifying the farming of animals (pastoral farming) is harder to centralize than for grains, vegetables, etc (arable farming).

What's the answer? The language and labelling at retail level. All those thousands of meat categories in stores – the labelling on the packaging should go beyond a small symbol on the back. If those in the industry put their names/company names/a picture of the founders (or all three) on the packaging, then that company is accountable for the entire process, from birth to plate, including the farming, slaughter, butchery, recipe, packaging and regulations. Shouldn't it be that the producers are the ones who should be putting their name on it? Not a governing body for one part of it. And, importantly, shouldn't retail, as the final stage in the meat chain, take responsibility for their customers and their customers' questions by representing their own standards? It's no less responsibility for the farm and the slaughterhouse, as there is a vital trust between them and the retailer, and the retailer will not choose to work with them if they don't trust them (or will cease trading with them immediately if the trust is broken). It is not okay for the retailer to say, 'Not my fault' as happened in the UK with the 2013 horsemeat scandal. Any regulation or certification paperwork that means that the retailer can avoid taking responsibility for their customers themselves is massively detrimental.

What's really strange is that, in supermarkets' defence, they do put their name on it. The dominance of 'own label' branded lines on supermarket shelves is massive now and it suggests they should have the greatest accountability and liability of all, but these supermarket brands have become so completely dominated by the message of 'price' that any attempt to prioritize taste and principles in this branding is lost. These 'own label' products are produced by contract to third parties, who in turn source through third parties (does that make a ninth party?) and we're back to 'Not my fault,' and 'There's no way we could have known'… This is not good enough. Rather than national certificates for the rearing of the animals, let's put the accountability back on the retailers for selling it. It's a lot of pressure on them, but it's a more practical definition of who is the final gatekeeper for this control and the retailer is the only person to whom most consumers have access to be able to ask these questions.

If the retailer can simply say 'we know them and we trust them', this nicely sums up this agreement. If the retailer is going to put their name on the pack and take full accountability, they must meet the farmers, shake their hands and ask them the same questions that consumers will ask them.

Maybe it's impossible immediately and they can use a blueprint and a contract to get started with a farm, but I think retailers should meet every farmer from whom they buy meat. That's why mass-produced meat just isn't good enough – how is it possible to stock 3,000 shelves every single day and still know where the animals are from?

What if marketing was in charge of procurement and sourcing? Too often now, the marketing department is there for damage control, when the pressures of a price-driven modern food market make the brand and the message fall apart. What if the people who are responsible for the message and the brand, plus the sales team on the shop floor who need to answer their questions, what if they were in charge of where the contents of those packs are from? Wouldn't that be a better way around than the financial department delivering annual targets for increasing margin, volume and market share? We could put the responsibility back on the marketing departments, and then we'd see how hard it is to sell something you know isn't good enough.

The traceability question is also important to understand. If a retailer can say they source meat from 'farms across the country' (for me, this means the UK, but the same applies wherever the retailer is). With further interest, they should be able to explain (and prove) that the animal was born, reared, slaughtered and processed in the UK. That's what I would call British meat. It's not just patriotism or investing in my own economy; it stands for another set of checks and regulations to help the retailer tell the customer that they trust the sourcing and they know where the meat is from. It's not to say that meat from other countries isn't just as good, or as well farmed, it is simply to demonstrate that the retailer knows the farms and knows how they get the meat to us. The same applies for American retailers or Australian or French and so on. If you can trace the meat to a number of farms in the same country, you can show that you know where it came from. Of course there are extreme examples: for example, a pig's carcass can be exported whole, but once a distribution wholesaler in the receving country removes the trotters, they are then permitted to say that the whole animal is the product of their country. This is an extreme, and there are mass suppliers that run checks and audits and strict sourcing regimes to import meat and who are not crooks, but it is being detached from the actual product that puts traceability at risk. Is it the marketing and sales team who are auditing the supply, ready to answer the questions properly? Almost certainly not unfortunately.

I'm not entirely naive, just an idealist and an optimist. Let's not move animals around so much while they're alive. Let's not move carcasses around so much when they're dead. A national meat supply is brilliant. It's challenging, expensive and (given the ticking clock of shelf life constantly chipping away at

your sanity) completely exhausting, but it can be a beautiful, admirable thing when it's done properly. In a small country like Britain, 'local' is a bonus but 'national' isn't usually more than about 300 miles away on average. In larger countries like Australia and America, using a similar geography to the one that humans use for their own sense of identity (regions or states, for example) is a pretty good start for working out how far your chilled/fresh food should travel. Again, I'm an idealist; it's not that I don't accept that the global food chain is out there, I just want to question those little parts of it that I could understand if I just try.

And now on to the last of my four questions, and the one that leads (seamlessly!) into the collection of cuts and recipes for this book...

WHAT DO I DO WITH IT?

This is my favourite question because it really covers all the other questions. When someone asks what to do with a piece of a meat, they're showing an interest in the taste, where it's from, what the price is, and whether it's 'good meat'. People asking this question are looking for more than a microwave lasagne or a pack of deli ham. To come to a meat shop and ask for cooking ideas is the start of a celebration of the taste of meat and nothing makes me happier than seeing that.

First and foremost, I like to eat meat. Which is why so far we've looked at what makes up our 'taste' response and hopefully have some ideas to help find our principles and priorities. However, more than this, I like to cook with meat as well as simply eat it. I like what a plate of different food becomes when one of the components is good meat, and I love the endless ideas and possibilities for cooking with it. That the same pig can be used to make anything from sausages needing 5 minutes to cook to a bone-in pulled pork shoulder (page 164) taking 4 hours to cook is amazing.

So to the question, 'What do I do with it?', I would respond with, 'How much time do you have to cook it?', because the possibilities and ideas are endless. And that's the idea with the recipe collection here – a lot of classic recipes and my takes on classic recipes, which are put into an order to hopefully suit how much time you have to cook them.

Our modern meat kitchens are busy places, with ovens, microwaves, food processors, freezers... Not to mention tablets, televisions and mobile/cell phones... We cook and eat in a totally different environment from 40 years ago and, literally, millennia removed from when we started to eat meat in the first place. Though the wonderful thing is that the practice is still essentially the same. We do, fundamentally, follow the same cycle of sleeping and eating to fuel ourselves.

Look how the methods of Western medical science have transformed because of inventions and discoveries in recent history; how feats of engineering and design have revolutionized the way we can travel in cars, planes and trains; how the invention of the phone completely flipped how we communicate, let alone the way we shop and pay for food, with the development of credit cards, the internet, and so on.

But we still, 1.9 million years later, cook and eat meat. There is no reason for any of us, even a cooking novice or someone who has never eaten meat before, not to have the confidence to handle meat as part of this history. When it comes to cooking meat, all this practice has made us really, really good at it, and when it comes to cutting and preparing meat for cooking, we already have all the basic instincts and capabilities that we need to be able to do it (I will show this later).

More than anything I've ever been taught, confidence has been the most valuable. I'm pretty sure that confidence means you can do about 90 per cent of anything in the world and 100 per cent with a lot of training and practice on top. The same goes for cooking, especially for cooking meat. So I'm going to start with a quick list of some general and practical dos and don'ts – the don'ts have been learned from my own valuable mistakes – to start our celebration of cooking and eating good meat and building our confidence to know what to do with it.

DOS	DON'TS
✱ Do buy a meat thermometer; they're not just for dads and BBQs, they're brilliant for getting the consistency of the meat right. ✱ Do get your hands in – we have nails (claws!) and opposable thumbs. There is nothing better for stripping the cold leftovers of roast chicken than our hands. Buy some disposable latex food gloves – they're so cheap and great for handling meat, and you'll never again think twice about handling garlic, onion or smoked salmon either. ✱ Do seal meat well before freezing. The best way to stop 'freezer burn' (when the moisture crystallizes) is to dry it with paper towels and wrap it tightly in clingfilm/plastic wrap or a sandwich bag. ✱ Do keep some chorizo or other cured meats in your fridge. Curing is the simplest way (as our ancestors learnt) to keep meat for longer and makes a tasty addition to recipes, especially if you haven't had time for a fresh food shop. ✱ Do try offal. I'm not a fan of liver, even after trying it a few times, I just don't love it on its own (though I like it in haggis and faggots), but I think heart and lungs/lights are great when available. And… ✱ …do serve 'fries' (testicles, also known as 'Rocky Mountain oysters', 'prairie oysters' and 'cowboy caviar') at a dinner party, just once! ✱ Do ask for opinions on food, but remember that, as we all eat, we all have a very different set of tastes. If you ask someone for an opinion, they will (out of goodness) give you one, even if they didn't actually have one until you asked. ✱ Do rest meat – it's nothing more complicated than letting the temperature drop a little, the meat relax and the small veins of fat thicken a little so that our taste buds can detect them better. Serve meat warm, not piping hot. ✱ Do sharpen your knives regularly; it makes preparing your meals more of a pleasure.	✱ Don't be embarrassed to order your steak well done if you like it that way. There's a strange culture that rarer meat is more sophisticated. It's just a different cooking time and flavour. ✱ Don't trim the fat. Keep it on for cooking, even if you don't eat it. Try cooking the edge of a sirloin steak or the rind of bacon for longer so that it becomes crispy. It's a totally different product from the lean muscle and can be just as delicious cooked to your taste. If you don't like the taste, don't be shy to leave it on the plate. ✱ Don't watch YouTube videos of abattoirs; there are so few videos of good abattoirs, it will completely skew your view. ✱ Don't worry if you're not fully on board with a media campaign for food. They are not dishonest or misleading, but they are produced by a television company whose audience data might not include you. Better to make lots of tiny ripples with your better meat purchases than wait to find the time to campaign. ✱ Don't only assign the the phrase 'processed meat' to cheap food. Grinding a well farmed rump steak is still classified as 'processed'. ✱ Don't be scared of salt. Too much is bad for you, but a sprinkle on meat you're cooking will largely dissolve and remain in the dish/pan. It's better to use salt for cooking than add salt to cooked food. Find salt with the strongest flavour and then you'll use less as well. ✱ Don't forget to taste with your nose – it's the best translator of flavour. If you're cooking a meat dish like a ragù and you hold dried basil up to your nose, your nose will tell you if you want to put it in more effectively than tasting the dried basil. The smell is the best indicator of the contributing flavour for a recipe. ✱ Don't forget kitchen foil to catch the juices and grease from roasting meat. If you're scouring away at your roasting pan every time, you'll be less excited to start the next recipe.

Most importantly, please remember...

...that there is no perfect taste. There are popular tastes, cuisines and dishes, but there is no single perfect taste. Food awards are helpful promotional tools, but there is such a fallacy that anything is the 'best tasting'... there is no such thing. There is only 'My favourite...' and everyone has a their own. Otherwise, there would be one film at the movies, one song in the charts, one item on a menu, and so on.

So, the reason I say this is because it is very hard to completely fail when making food for yourself or for guests. There will always be things – flavourings, seasoning, cooking time – that you might do differently next time, but it's hard to fail completely, and the worst possible outcome is that you have to serve something else (that's why I like to keep leftovers in the freezer!). Is that so bad? In the pursuit of confidence, will you agree to these four things?

1. You will always start with 'good meat' (following the parameters we have covered), which makes it so much harder to fail.

2. You will treat this collection of recipes as a guide and adapt them in any way you like. They're ideas, some classic and conservative and some a bit different and more adventurous, but they are just ideas to try. Shake them up with anything that you know you like or take out the things you don't.

3. You will remember that I'm a home cook, not professionally trained. I made recipes first as a hobby and then as a business, where all of my product development is down to trial, error and customer feedback. The error is the most helpful part of the process, and though you want to avoid error 5 minutes before dinner guests arrive, don't be afraid to try something different when you aren't under pressure.

4. You will, on presenting a recipe to anyone else, accompany it with the words, 'There. Nailed it!' Nothing excites the sensory reaction and anticipation of the taste buds more than confident presentation – it's the foundation of all food packaging and brand design. After years of celebrity chefs, television shows and so many experts in food, we've lost the ability to sit down for a meal without first listing a) whose recipe it is b) what went wrong c) what went wrong last time we tried it d) miscellaneous list of things for which we should apologize. We just don't need to do it. Our grandparents would have never dreamed of discussing whether the food was any good, and not out of stifled courtesy, just because there was no chink in the armour of confidence from the person who made it. Imagine if there was a bottle of wine on the shelf and the label said, 'You can buy this but I have to say that it's not our best year. Last year's was better. I'm not really sure why, but I think it was that we kept the grapes on the vines a little bit longer. So, anyway, drink up but just remember, it's not our best.' Nobody would buy it. If they did, they wouldn't enjoy it because not only has it failed to trigger the taste buds, the salivation, the anticipation, it's completely turned them off.

If I can leave you with one skill, beyond butchering your own pork shoulder or filleting your own chicken, it's to present the plates of your culinary creation with total pride, even a little smugness. The effect this will have on the tastes and eating experience of your dining companions is wonderful. And if they still don't like it... well, it's just their tastebuds. And there's nothing you can do about that!

So, now, to what to do with it...

COOKTCHERY

'Cooktchery' is a term I use for cutting meat at home. Essentially it is butchery for cooking, rather than retail.

Skilled and trained butchery is a beautiful thing to watch – the effortless flow and controlled pace of an experienced butcher cutting down some meat is utterly mesmerizing. It is, however, a craft for a profession and it has been developed for two main reasons: the commercial value of using the maximum amount of meat on a carcass and achieving the best presentation to appeal to customers.

There is no value to a meat retailer for muscle that is sliced in a way that it can't be sold on its own. Minced/ground and cubed meat makes the best use of all the trim, even the small pieces around the bones. It's worth mentioning the ethical position with this as well: if you're wasting a single piece of meat, you are not honouring the life of the animal.

This is not to say that I endorse the process of mechanically reclaimed meat, which captures every single 'non-bone' part in the manufacture of 'pink slime'. This process uses machines to strip every piece off a carcass and then another machine to pulverise it until it's edible, which is far from butchery. But what I most object to is the result being sold as 'meat'. Commercially skilled butchery will use every part of the muscle, as well as the offal and the 'fifth quarter' for by-products, and it will be sold as such, too.

The other reason for trained butchery is to present meat attractively, which shows care and precision and inspires trust in the product. If it doesn't look good, our brains will not send the signals that we want to eat it, our 'mental accounting' (page 16) will put this at a lower value than its price tag and we won't buy it. We shop with our eyes – it's not just marketing speak.

However, cutting a piece or joint of meat in your own home isn't the same as cutting it for retail. You don't need to worry about the cumulative cost of a few grams/ounces of meat going to waste on 1,000 carcasses in a month, for example, and you don't need to worry that it's looking perfect for retail. You're simply going to cook it.

So let's start doing a bit of cutting ourselves in our own kitchens. We already do this when we trim a bit of rind on bacon or remove the skin on chicken breasts, for example. If it's any interest to you to take it a step further, you'll see that's it really easy, very satisfying and (to suit our modern lives and budgets), much better value than pre-packaged cuts.

And you won't be surprised to hear me say again, if you start with 'good meat' you simply can't go wrong. Butchery for the purpose of cooking is wonderfully easy, I promise.

We're going to do a rib of beef, a leg of lamb, a shoulder of pork and a whole chicken. The chicken is interesting because chicken is the most price-pressured meat in the world. There is so much of a range in its pricing that it is difficult to know what is the 'right' price for chicken. Indeed, people always ask why 'good chicken' is so expensive, when they should be asking why cheap chicken is so cheap, so as well as listing the processes involved in cutting it down into pieces, I'll have a go at explaining the cost savings you'll make here, too.

WHAT YOU WILL NEED TO BE A HOME 'COOKTCHER':

These are all available with a quick internet search, or ask your butcher or local meat shop if you can source some equipment through them.

Butcher's twine

Paring knife

Chef's knife (larger, all purpose kitchen knife, ideally with a bit of weight to it and more than 15-cm/6-inch length of blade)

Knife sharpener

Scissors

Cutting board

Muslin/cheesecloth (optional)

Meat saw (optional)

Boning knife (optional – quite like the paring knife for getting into small cuts but more flexible to be able to bend around the bones and joints)

COOKTCHERY TIPS

Here are a few cooking hints and tips that will help you become a successful and confident cooktcher!

Rolling with twine

The stronger the twine or string, the easier and better. Red and white (or blue and white) butcher's twine is best.

Simply explained, you need to tie the meat back together after you've boned it. You can make individual ties: cut a piece of twine, wrap it under the meat, tie it on top tightly with a double knot, then trim the ends. And repeat. If you're doing this, it's easiest to start in the middle of the piece of meat to hold the centre together (the first knot is always the hardest), then do the next one to the right and to the left, and then back to the right, etc. The benefit of this style is that you can string a whole piece of meat and then cut it down into smaller pieces between the strings. Also, as you can imagine for a butcher, this helps them roll a larger piece and then cut it down at the customer's request without having to retie it.

However, the other way to tie, which I find easier, can be used if you don't need to cut the meat down to a smaller size. Tie the first piece of twine at one end (I tend to go left to right), tie it tightly with a double knot. Then run the twine around the outside of the cut of meat 2 cm/1 inch along. Next you need to bring it back over the top, but use your finger to pull back the join of the twine that's attached to the previous knot and thread the end between the twine and the meat – this creates a lever so that you can pull it tighter and with the tension from turning the meat away from you, it'll hold the string long enough for you to repeat the process at intervals along the stretch of the meat. You'll have a 'spine' of string along the base of the meat, so you'll see that you can't cut between the ties or you'll cut through this twine spine and it'll untie the whole lot. However, if you're just tying and 'cooktchering' for your own cooking (and you don't need to resize the piece of meat), it's a very easy way of tying.

Tunnel boning

As the name suggests, this is tunnelling out a bone. It is, for example, how you could get the bone out of a pork leg without having to cut a line down the middle to reach the bone and open out the meat. It's only recommended if you're going to slow cook the piece of meat. This is because, by tunnelling in from either end with a knife until the bone can be twisted out, you get a neat and tidy result but you haven't had access to the sinews and tissue inside, so you won't have trimmed it back to lean muscle. Therefore a fast, dry roast will mean that the 'chewy' bits inside don't have a chance to dissolve and tenderize.

Sharpening your knife

My favourite method of sharpening a knife is by using a 'steel' (a handled, long rod of metal). A sharp knife makes everything easier. A butcher will have their steel by them (or connected to their belt) and will do three quick sharpens every 10–15 slices of meat. It becomes a habit and keeps the knife razor-sharp. I hold the steel with the tip down and the weight of my arm holding the handle in place and then run the blade of the knife either side of the steel, just a few times. The best advice I can give you is to keep playing with it. Wait until it sounds right and feels satisfying. Have a lemon nearby, as that's great for testing for sharpness (and cheaper than slashing up a piece of meat). If you pinch your thumbnail on the blade edge too, you'll hear a click on a ridge one way and feel a rounded curve on the other side. There is a dominant side to your knife – don't worry about this too much, but if you do two strokes on the soft side and one on the ridge side, you'll have a sharp knife in three strokes.

Hand-cutting and cubing

Cubing is very simple. The longer you're going to cook the meat, the less you need to trim it, as the tissue and proteins will break down in the liquid (for example in a cassoulet or stew). However, if you're using diced meat for a shorter or dry cooking process (for example in a stir-fry), trim off all the fats and sinew so that you just have lean meat, as the strips or cubes of meat won't have long enough to tenderize.

Mincing/grinding seems like something that needs a mincer/grinder but it really isn't more complicated than finely dicing an onion, for example. Just keep slicing it until it's in really small pieces. You'll get to experience a wonderfully different texture and flavour with hand-cut mince in dishes like Spaghetti Bolognese or Chilli Con Carne. If you're cutting it for burgers, meatballs or meatloaf, try and go even more fine so that it binds together well.

MEAT AND POULTRY COOKING GUIDES

RED MEAT

As a general guide for all red meat (beef, veal, lamb, mutton, venison and pork), I plan for around 250 g/9 oz. of boneless meat per person (a little more for bigger appetites) and 350–400 g/12–13 oz. to allow for bone-in roasts, so that it yields the same amount of boneless meat.

If you're serving a lot of accompaniments (chips or roasted vegetables with a steak, for example), then reduce the weight of the meat a little to 225 g/8 oz. For beef sirloin though, for example, with the lovely spine of fat down the side, keep in mind that you or your guest might not eat this part and, although it is essential for flavour in the cooking, you might look for a slightly thicker-cut steak to compensate for how much might be left on the plate.

Roasting

Unless stated in a recipe, roasting is always uncovered, in a roasting pan, on the middle shelf of the oven, usually turned halfway or basted with the juices from the pan.

You'll see in some of the roasting recipes in this book, there's a lovely benefit from 'browning'. Do this by either heating a pan with a little oil or butter and turning the meat in it for a few minutes to 'sear' the edges, or preheat your oven to 200°C (400°F) Gas 6 and start cooking the roast, whatever its weight, unwrapped, for 15 minutes at this temperature. Then begin the usual cooking following the temperatures and timings opposite.

The temperatures are recommended for preheated ovens. I didn't appreciate the value of this until I started to adhere to it; it's not just to count the minutes properly, it has a better effect on the meat to put it into a hot oven rather than a cold oven that only heats up slowly with the joint already in there.

Braising and pot-roasting

For braising and pot-roasting, it's similar proportionally, just a lot lower and slower. This method is great for rolled beef brisket, boneless leg of lamb ('butterflied lamb'), boneless leg or 'haunch' of venison, and any cuts that need long, slow, moist cooking to tenderize them.

Pan-frying and griddling

This quick cooking method is for cooking steaks, medallions, tournedos, chops, cutlets, fillets, etc. The guide opposite is based on 2-cm/1-inch thick steaks, but you will need to increase the times for thicker cuts and take note of the visual and 'prod' test to keep an eye on it. Although you can cook beef and lamb steaks rare, you should make sure that pork is cooked through.

Like the importance of pre-heating an oven before roasting, the secret to pan-frying is to get the pan really hot before putting the piece in. This browns or 'sears' the outside straight away, which produces a lovely, soft, burnt, caramelized flavour.

POULTRY AND FEATHER GAME

For whole smaller birds (chicken, duck, guinea fowl, pheasant, partridge, etc.) the United States Department of Agriculture (USDA) Food Safety and Inspection Service (FSIS) recommends cooking whole chicken to a safe minimum internal temperature of 74°C (165°F). Check the temperature using a thermometer in the inner part of the thigh and the thickest part of the breast. You should also check the colour of the meat juices. When you've followed the cooking guide opposite, remove the chicken from the oven, scratch the surface of the thickest bit of the leg and press down with a fork. If the juices are still pink, it needs longer in the oven. Test it again after 10 minutes and repeat if necessary.

RED MEAT ROASTING TIMES

Target	Oven temp	Cooking time per 1 kg/2¼ lbs.	Meat temp
Rare	190°C (375°F)	30 minutes	55°C (130°F)
Medium	180°C (350°F)	45 minutes	65°C (150°F)
Well done	180°C (350°F)	55 minutes	72°C (162°F)

RED MEAT BRAISING AND POT-ROASTING TIMES

Target	Oven temp	Cooking time per 1 kg/2¼ lbs.	Meat temp
Tender	160°C (325°F)	60 minutes	55°C (130°F)
Melt-in-the-mouth	145°C (275°F)	80 minutes	65°C (150°F)
Seriously tender melt-in-the-mouth	130°C (250°F)	90 minutes	65°C (150°F)

RED MEAT PAN-FRYING AND GRIDDLING TIMES

Target	Hob temp	Cooking time	Visual and 'prod' test
Rare	Mark 6	2 minutes either side	Brown coating but still very soft when you prod it. The fats will still be light and soft.
Medium	Mark 6 then turn down to Mark 3	2 minutes either side then a further 2 minutes either side	Brown all over. Any fat will be brown and starting to crisp. It will be a little harder when you prod it, like pressing your eyeball through your eyelid.
Well done	Mark 6 then turn down to Mark 3	2 minutes either side then a further 3 minutes either side	Very dark brown all over. All fats brown and crispy and reduced in size. *Much harder to prod, like pressing the tips of your finger and thumb together.

POULTRY AND FEATHER GAME ROASTING TIMES

Bird	Oven temp	Cooking time per 1 kg/2¼ lbs.	Meat temp
Small whole birds (chicken, duck, guinea fowl, etc.)	190°C (375°F)	40 minutes	74°C (165°F)
Larger birds (turkey, capon, etc.)	190°C (375°F)	45 minutes	74°C (165°F)
Whole turkey up to 6 kg/ 13 lbs. (unstuffed weight)	190°C (375°F)	30 minutes	74°C (165°F)
Whole turkey 6–11 kg/ 13–24 lbs. (stuffed weight)	200°C (400°F) for 25 minutes then 190°C (375°F)	30 minutes	74°C (165°F)

COOKING STYLES

Braising

For 'thicker', more protein-rich cuts, such as beef brisket, this cooking method uses liquid in a sealed pan to cook the meat slowly with maximum moisture. These guidelines should help you braise a piece of meat to perfection:

1 Preheat the oven according to the table on page 29.

2 Heat a little butter in a flameproof casserole with a lid and brown the outside of the piece of meat for 2 minutes.

3 Remove the joint and set aside for a moment. Add a little more butter to the casserole, if needed, and then cook some chopped onions, carrots and celery (known as a 'mirepoix') in the butter until softened. This will give you the base.

4 Place the browned meat on top of the base and pour in enough stock to submerge the joint, probably around 750 ml–1 litre/3–4 cups.

5 See the braising timings in the table on page 29 and calculate the timing for your weight and desired consistency. Cook in the preheated oven according to these timings and temperatures.

6 This is an optional stage. Work out the half-way stage of cooking. At this time, remove the meat for a moment and strain the liquid. Discard the vegetables and pour a little of the liquid stock (about 2 cm/1 inch deep) back into the pan, put the joint of meat back in and return to the oven. Pour the rest of the liquid stock into another pan and boil hard on the hob until it reduces and thickens. Meanwhile, keep turning and basting the meat every 15 minutes.

7 To serve, remove the joint to carve. Chill the stock for use another time or, if you've thickened the stock following step 6, serve it as a sauce to pour over the top of the carved meat. (Save any leftover sauce and chill in the fridge for jellied stock another time.)

Pot-roasting

This is very similar to braising but it uses less liquid, so it produces a drier, richer-flavoured meat, which might be a little less succulent. Therefore, if it's a lean piece of meat like venison or beef topside/silverside/round then a 'bard' is a great idea for cooking. (To 'bard' a piece of meat basically means to wrap or coat it in extra fat, such as bacon or pork fat.)

1 Preheat the oven according to the table on page 29.

2 Heat a little butter in an flameproof casserole with a lid and brown the outside of the piece of meat or the 'bard', if using, for 2 minutes.

3 Remove the joint and set aside for a moment. Add a little more butter to the casserole, if needed, and then cook some chopped onions, carrots and celery (the mirepoix) in the butter until softened. This will give you the base.

4 Place the browned meat on top of the base and pour in 2 cm/1 inch of stock to moisten.

5 See the pot-roasting timings in the table on page 29 and calculate the timing for your weight and desired consistency. Cook in the preheated oven according to these timings and temperatures.

6 Turn the joint halfway and baste with the liquid at the bottom of the casserole. If it's getting dry, add a little more water or stock.

7 To serve, remove the joint to carve. If you've added a bard, then cut that off and either fry it off in a pan to brown or pop it under the grill/broiler with a sprinkle of sea salt to crackle and offer it on the side.

Grilling

One for a barbecue/outdoor grill (or under a grill/broiler when the weather isn't ideal for a cook-out). Here are some general tips for cooking meat outdoors:

1 Preheating is very important. Make sure the barbecue/outdoor grill is really hot ('white hot') before putting meat on to cook. It's the best for searing the edges and helping the binding, particularly holding together things like burgers, and makes the most of that smoky flavour.

2 To make sure the middle of the pieces are cooked well or medium, make good use of a lid or cover. So sear the meat over high heat first, then put the lid down to intensify the temperature and help cook through to the middle. Gas or electric barbecues/outdoor grills can be controlled to reduce the temperature a bit at this stage too or, for charcoal, move the meat to the sides or away from the hottest section of coals.

3 Don't turn meat too quickly, especially for tender pieces and minced/ground products like burgers. Let them sit for 2 minutes first so they cook through on the one side. Constantly turning runs the risk of breaking them up or damaging the surface too much. Have the confidence to let them sit for at least 2 minutes to start with.

4 Don't use forks to turn, try and use soft tongs. There isn't a pan or dish below to catch the meat juices so we want to keep as much in the meat as possible.

5 Avoid using lighter fuel or firestarters, as they'll add a rather toxic taste to the meat.

6 Keep a meat thermometer handy, if you have one. Meat cooked on a barbecue/outdoor grill can be the trickiest to test and you need to make sure that chicken and pork are fully cooked through.

Boiling

This is simply placing a piece of meat into water or stock and lightly simmering (rather than actually boiling). It's a great way to tenderize thicker cuts of meat like a horseshoe gammon/ham (see Honey and Mustard Ham Hocks, page 208) or a rolled breast of lamb.

Poaching

This is very similar to boiling and can be used for the same process, but it is often used specifically for submerging a wrapped piece of meat in water (either covering or sitting in a few cm/inches of liquid) and then lightly simmering until cooked. (See Poached Whole Ballotine Chicken with Basil Pesto, page 139.)

Sautéing

This method of cooking is good if you want to keep meat pieces quite rare. Heat a little oil or butter in a frying pan/skillet and just brown until the outside of the pieces of meat are browned. (Remove the meat if you need to use the pan to sauté vegetables or make a sauce, then pop the meat pieces back in to reheat to serve.)

Stir-frying

This is the same process as above, but the meat is fully cooked through and you can fry the other vegetables with it. Start with garlic and onions before the meat so that the meat absorbs those flavours, then add the other ingredients.

Chargrilling and griddling

These cooking methods are lovely for attractive presentation, particularly for steaks, as the strips/grates of heat singes dark lines across the meat, but this also adds a lovely caramelized flavour. It's a great way to keep the meat rare, while also crisping up the surface.

1 Get the griddle pan smoking hot and use just a little oil (or not at all if the pan is non-stick).

2 Place the meat (steaks or chicken breasts work well) into the griddle pan.

3 Don't turn too quickly, let them sear and acquire the dark markings along the meat.

4 Turn them over to sear the other side.

5 If the first side needs more time, try and turn to match the angle of the lines again (although this is just a presentation thing!).

WHITE CHICKEN STOCK

This is distinct from Brown Chicken Stock – it is a simpler, shorter option that doesn't include roasting the carcass first. If you're cutting your own whole chicken, follow the instructions to debone it on page 70.

1.5 litres/2²/₃ pints water
1 white onion, chopped
2 garlic cloves (optional), chopped
1 carrot, chopped
2 celery sticks, chopped
1 bay leaf
a big pinch of black pepper
1 teaspoon whole pink peppercorns
carcass of 1 whole chicken

MAKES ABOUT 150 ML/²/₃ CUP

Bring the water to the boil in a pan with a lid. Then add the vegetables, bay leaf, black pepper and peppercorns and return to the boil.

Add the chicken carcass and then reduce the heat to a simmer and leave to cook over low heat, covered, for 3 hours. Occasionally, skim the surface. You can just use a sieve/strainer or some paper towels to run over the top of the water.

After 3 hours, strain the liquid into a bowl and allow to cool. Once it's at room temperature, transfer it to the fridge. Keep chilled for up to 8 days or freeze in portions (a good tip is to use an ice cube tray, which means you can just defrost as much as you need in future).

BROWN CHICKEN STOCK

The 'brown' here refers to roasting the chicken bones before making the stock. I think it adds an oaky flavour and makes it perfect with red meat dishes. If you're cutting your own whole chicken, this will use all the bones (see pages 69–70).

carcass of 1 whole chicken
1 white onion, roughly chopped
1 carrot, roughly chopped
1 celery stick, roughly chopped
2 garlic cloves, roughly chopped
1 bay leaf
a big pinch of black pepper
2 tablespoons olive oil
1.5 litres/2²/₃ pints water

MAKES ABOUT 250 ML/1 CUP

Preheat the oven to 180°C (350°F) Gas 4.

Place the chicken bones in a roasting pan, scatter the vegetables around and add the bay leaf and pepper. Drizzle the olive oil on top and roast, uncovered, in the preheated oven for 30 minutes.

Bring the water to the boil in a pan with a lid. Add the contents of your roasting pan. Reduce the heat to a simmer and cook over low heat, covered, for at least 3 hours. Occasionally, skim the surface. You can just use a sieve/strainer or some paper towels to run over the top of the water.

Strain the liquid into a bowl and allow to cool. Once it's at room temperature, transfer it to the fridge to help it turn to a jelly consistency. Cover and keep in the fridge up to 1 week or freeze in portions (use an ice-cube tray, so you can just defrost as much as you need in future).

BEEF BROTH

For a really hearty nutritious broth or to chill and use as stock, this is such an easy throw-in-a-pan-for-another-time recipe or something to make as a large batch and portion for the freezer. As with the Brown Chicken Stock, we're going to roast the bones first to release the goodness in the marrow and enhance the flavours.

1 beef bone (or the ribs from the rib, see pages 45–47)

800 g/3½ cups cubed beef

100 g/⅔ cup chopped streaky/fatty bacon

2 tablespoons olive oil

30 g/2 tablespoons butter

1 white onion, roughly chopped

1 garlic clove, roughly chopped

1 carrot, unpeeled and roughly chopped

1 parsnip, unpeeled and roughly chopped

1 celery stick, roughly chopped

a big pinch of black pepper

1 bay leaf

a pinch of dried thyme or a sprig of fresh

3 litres/12 cups water

1 tablespoon plain/all-purpose flour (optional)

**MAKES ABOUT 400 ML/
¾ PINT OR SERVES 2
AS A SOUP**

Preheat the oven to 180°C (350°F) Gas 4.

Put the bone, cubed beef and bacon in a roasting pan, drizzle the olive oil over the top and roast in the preheated oven for 25 minutes.

Meanwhile, heat the butter in a large pan on the hob. Add the onion, garlic, carrot, parsnip and celery and cook for 5 minutes.

Add the pepper, bay leaf and thyme, then pour in the water and bring to the boil.

If you want to serve this as a soup with meaty chunks in it, rather than a liquid broth, keep half the beef and bacon pieces to the side after roasting to add later. Place the rest (or all) of the contents of the roasting pan into the water, reduce the heat to a simmer and cook over low heat, covered, for up to 3 hours.

Occasionally, skim the surface. You can just use a sieve/strainer or some paper towels to run over the top of the water.

Strain the liquid into a clean pan. Either serve it as it is, as a lovely, rich broth or add the reserved beef and bacon back in with the flour and heat through until thickened. Alternatively, allow to cool to room temperature then transfer to the fridge for up to 1 week or freeze in portions (use an ice-cube tray, so you can just defrost as much as you need in future).

BEEF

I don't believe there is a better meat than beef to demonstrate good farming – and of course, by contrast, poor farming. My top meat-eating experiences have all been beef, and if I had to choose just one meat for the rest of my life, it would be beef. I'll cover a lot about general livestock in this beef section, as I did on pages 10–11 because the qualities and practices of beef farming extend to most handling of other livestock. I find beef is the best general case study for red meat, and I hope you'll allow me to use the considerations here as the reference for the subsequent veal, lamb and pork sections too.

'The feeling of friendship is like that of being comfortably filled with roast beef....' SAMUEL JOHNSON

If we're going to track the role of meat in our evolution, we need to go back to our Neolithic ancestors (between 10,000 and 6,500 years ago). This was when the domestication of animals was developed, and cattle, particularly towards the end of this period, were a massively significant part of this 'agricultural revolution'. This is when we became farmers, not hunters, and we tamed the wild auroch into our control. It was their domestication that evolved into what we have as cattle today. Incidentally the word cattle comes from the Anglo-French word 'chattel', meaning 'possession'. By this stage, we are now owning animals, not hunting wild ones.

Not to get too bogged down in anthropology, but this move to farming made us settlers. We no longer had to travel to find our fuel – we could keep our food with us. With settled lives, we developed society and culture, as well as the responsibility of a live food source. This was the start of animal husbandry. Maybe that's why live animals are so impressive to us still today, and why to butcher and handle raw meat always feels, to me, like an honour.

BEEF FOR BEGINNERS

For the cook in our modern meat kitchen, there is no greater head start than a good bit of beef (steak, minced/ground beef, roasting cut or cubed). It's the meat that you can worry about the least in terms of cooking time, succulence and flavour, as it is perfectly structured and balanced to offer the 'whole package' for eating experience. From a practical point of view, it's also got the longest chilled shelf life, it holds up pretty well in the freezer, it has a great range of uses for its by-products, and the structure of it (meat to bone ratio) makes it much more straightforward to butcher. Though it seems like a whole fore-rib/rib section might be a daunting place to begin one's first attempt at butchery, it's an awful lot easier than the tighter design of, for example, lamb shoulder, where sinews, muscle and bones are far more tightly packed together, fiddly and more prone to shards and chips. So, as we'll do in a moment, starting with a hunk of beef is actually the best place to start building up our meat-handling skills.

THE SCIENCE OF COLOUR

Beef is a naturally dense muscle, made up of water, fats and protein (as is all muscle), but it undergoes an exciting process of change from slaughter, through ageing and cooking that makes it a masterclass in biology, food science and the pursuit of great-tasting food. Not to go too much into this (as I'm afraid I would still find myself out of my depth), but visible colour changes are a key indicator of the taste quality of the meat. More so than any other meat, the high myoglobin (the deep-red iron- and oxygen-holding protein) demonstrates the quality and tenderness of the piece of meat. Even a small amount of hanging after slaughter (at minimum to chill the carcass to a safe temperature before cutting), will show this protein start to break down and dull in colour. Hanging/ageing further will see this dull more every day. And finally, when you come to cook the piece of beef, what can start as still 'red' becomes a brown-grey, as the myoglobin breaks down completely.

I mention this example of the life of the piece of meat because, contrary to popular belief and marketing, bright red meat is not always fresher. Indeed, when you take a piece of meat out of packaging, or if you mince/grind it, it will become, for a short period, bright red again due the contact that it has with the oxygen in the air. Oxygen-flushing or 'gas-flushing' was developed to pump pure oxygen into the sealed pack to keep the meat pink, but it doesn't indicate the freshness of the meat. It doesn't do any harm and it's a helpful tool for increasing shelf-life, but I just want to mention it so that you have the knowledge to make informed decisions. The discolouring of the myoglobin is a natural occurrence and not an indicator of 'old meat'.

TENDERNESS

The number-one quality people desire with beef is tenderness. This isn't a recipe requirement or a food trend, it's simply the enjoyment that the majority of us have when we have a piece of beef that doesn't need sawing and chewing. Here are the questions to ask your butcher to have the best chance of tender beef:

1. Do you like the abattoir or slaughterhouse? Meat retailers should have all witnessed the slaughter of our meat supply; it is not a huge ask and it's fundamental to the accountability that they must have for your meat supply. What this question asks is: was the animal stressed when it was killed? As I've mentioned, a worried animal will flood adrenalin into its muscle if it's scared. If I came into the room you're in now, slammed my hand down on the table and shouted your name, you would feel a physical surge of adrenalin through your muscles, particularly right to the ends of your arms and legs. This is to enable you to either fight me or run like the wind and, though I'm not scary or actually attacking you, you can't control it. And neither can other mammals; it's a fundamental element in our survival. Then, when you have the next split second to see that it's just me, your brain will send the follow signal to your adrenal glands to say, 'It's okay, false alarm, it's just Miranda trying to prove a point' and the adrenalin leaves the muscles. What happens when the mammal is slaughtered is that the brain can't follow up with this release and the adrenalin never leaves the muscles. Clench your fist now and see the difference in the strength of your forearm, then imagine that that never unclenches. Therefore, what is best for the animal is also best for the product.

2. How old is it? This question covers three things: the age of the animal, the shelf life and the ageing, and I'll quickly cover these three points and their role in our beef cooking and eating experience. Firstly the age of the beef cow or steer when it was slaughtered is relevant to taste and tenderness because of how much the animal has moved around. The older the animal, the more it has used its muscles and the more the connective tissues have grown and strengthened. Without intervention, a piece of 18-month-old animal's beef will be more tender than that of a 30-month-old animal. However, there is a point in an animal's life where the age and the yield of the animal meet for the most sustainable but viable commercial balance. By this, I mean that if an animal is not fully grown, it is small. Therefore you don't get as much meat from it or, of course, as much money for the animal. The price paid for the whole animal on a per kg/lb. calculation for the weight and grade of its yield would be less than for a fully grown animal. That difference, across a herd of 100 or 1,000 cattle is a massive factor for a farm's income and business.

At the same time, we need to find the balance between what is best for the animal and for the business. It honours the life of the animal far more to slaughter it once it can yield the most it can produce, rather than to slaughter it before maturity. What was the purpose of its life if you didn't produce everything you could? It would be like harvesting a field of wheat when the 'ear' is only half grown. The older age does have some cost to the tenderness and flavour of the meat though, so that's why ageing, butchery and cooking come into play to tenderize and further finish the beef.

Secondly, shelf life is pretty straightforward across all foods as everything is eventually perishable. Simply put, when the level of bacteria has overcome the piece of food, it is bad for us to eat it. We have bacteria around and inside us all the time, and most of it is harmless. However, bacteria develops as fast as it can, which is why humans have invented salt-curing, smoking, fridges, freezers, post-pack-pasteurizing, aluminium cans, heat-sealing, gas-flushing, vac-packing, etc. All of these techniques and products developed to fend off the inevitable triumph of bacteria over our food. So asking, 'How old is it?' is a great way to ask how many more days you will be able to keep it in your fridge until they would recommend you eat it safely. This will be based on microbiological testing in the labs as well as

sensory (sight, taste and smell) experience over the years. You are totally right to ask for the longest possible shelf life, but also please remember that if you're eating it that night, shelf life is, indeed, still 'life' and the cost of all food products in the world will go down if we are more willing to buy products with just enough life for when we plan to eat them, rather than longer. In other words, if you're not planning to eat it until next Thursday, of course ask if there is a newer product with enough life, but if you're planning to eat it that night, there is no need for the longer life. Indeed (as we'll look at next) your beef, if it's 'good meat', will be better towards the end of its commercial shelflife anyway.

Lastly, on to ageing, though to define what is 'better' in the case of ageing beef is a little tricky, because tastebuds, like snowflakes are all different. However, some understanding of ageing can really help you pick the best beef, in terms of tenderness in particular, if you ask the right questions about it.

A popular and somewhat trendy (or perhaps 'marketable') process is dry-ageing. This basically means leaving the meat on the carcass in a fridge for a period of time after slaughter. You have to hang it for a minimum of 2 days to reduce the temperature and see out rigor mortis (another process that causes tension in the muscles, but this one dissipates). But ageing it for longer than a couple of days means that a process naturally occurs in the meat. It accumulates lactic acid, which has the effect of reducing the pH, helping some of the protein present in the muscle to break down. It doesn't break down the connective tissues, but it tenderizes the meat and small protein fibres around them.

There is plenty of debate about the best length of time to dry-age meat, and the benefits of dry-ageing over wet-ageing (which is vacuum-sealing the meat in a plastic bag and keeping it in the fridge). It's a long and complex study of individual preferences and commercial gains but, for what it's worth, my preferred experience is that it is dry-aged on the bone for up to 2 weeks and then it doesn't seem to matter if it's vacuum-sealed for a short amount of time after that and, indeed, I would rather meat is transported in sealed, labelled bags for cleanliness and traceability. I recommend removing a cut joint or steak from a sealed bag for at least 20 minutes before cooking, for the simple reason that the blood and moisture coating the steak will be the first thing to cook and add an iron/metallic taste to the meat.

I will (yet again!) cite the distinction between 'good' meat and 'cheap' meat, as you could add all the trimmings and mod-cons to a Fiat but it still wouldn't be an Aston Martin... Asking if the butcher likes the farm is going to tell you yet more.

3. Do you like the farm? So as I keep mentioning throughout this book, good farming is the key to good meat. Our friends and fantastic suppliers of British cured meats at Trealy Farm in Monmouthshire helped me answer this question further. I asked, 'Given that curing meat is arguably the most handling one can do with a piece of meat...' (for salamis and chorizos, for example, this involves chopping up all the meat, turning it inside out, mixing it with salts and seasonings and then controlling the temperature for 40 days) '...do you believe that the most important part of any meat production, for eating experience, taste and succulence, is what happens to the animal when it's alive?"

They said, 'Yes'. That no matter how much cutting, cooking, curing, handling, processing, etc., is done, a commitment to starting with well-farmed raw meat will always result in a superior end product. In other words, back to my analogy, you can't make an Aston Martin out of a Fiat.

So the question for your butcher, 'Do you like the farm?' covers the rearing and all the stages

in the chronology on pages 10–11. The feeding is incorporated into this question too, unless you would prefer to ask about it separately. In other words, is it slowly or traditionally farmed? Or is it intensively farmed? Even more simply, did the animal eat what it wanted to eat and do what it wanted to do? If this sounds like a version of the question a 7-year-old might ask, it's because it is. When discussing meat with children I obviously don't go a lot into the farming and slaughter processes, although, incidentally, children, untarnished so far by sensationalized media, often bring me the most wonderfully inspiring reasoning and rational understanding of the practice of eating animals. Even in cities and suburbs, they are unoffended by a balance of life for the purpose of death. To arm them with an initial understanding, I ask them, 'What's your favourite food?' And they'll say something like, 'Spaghetti.' And I'll ask, 'What's your favourite game?" And they'll say something like, 'Football.' And then I'll say, 'Well, a cow's favourite food is grass, and her favourite thing to do is be in a field with her friends... so imagine if your teachers let you eat spaghetti whenever you wanted and play football whenever you wanted?' ... that usually does it! They're on board with good farming and know the most important question to ask of anyone selling meat – did the animal eat what it wanted to eat and did it do what it wanted to do during its lifetime?

Even better, animals (including humans) like to find their own food and to be in control of it. We don't like to be fed and we certainly wouldn't like to be force-fed. If you're a hunter and/or gatherer, your instinct is to feed yourself.

Cattle that are grass-fed have cleaner bodies alive and on the butcher's block. Feeding only grain and cereal (and worse) is not natural for the cattle's digestion. With many more years of this, they will evolve, but like many of the food-science advances made in producing commercially 'efficient' foods, we just can't process that food easily. So on a simple level at the slaughterhouse, a cereal- and grain-fed carcass has a dirty gut, and when the gut is removed, the e-coli and potentially harmful bacteria is released into the air and onto the floor. Now of course it is totally possible to control this and food standards and regulations ensure (or at least request) that this faecal matter doesn't contaminate the parts that continue on for meat, but it just isn't as simple to handle the carcass from a hygiene perspective.

Incidentally, I'm not a fan of Kobe and Wagyu beef. The marbling and tenderness is impressive, and it sounds like the animals are treated with care as they're regularly massaged, but they're 'encouraged' to eat as much grain and cereal as possible to produce the fats in the meat (the marbling). Also, although technically 'domesticated', the physical human handling of livestock is still unnatural to the animals. In other words, they're not eating what they want to eat and not doing what they want to do... Food should grow the skeleton, not just the muscle. You could feed a child nothing but chocolate bars and it would be huge, but it would be horrifically unhealthy. It's the same with animals. This leads us back to taste and principles. What is best for one, is undeniably better for the other.

UNDERSTANDING BEEF CUTS

Once you've identified which cut you've got and which part of the cow it's come from, it's time to work out how to get the most out of it.

The names, styles, butchery and cooking methods vary a little bit between countries, but the main approach is the same: if it's lean, cook it good and fast, and if it's fibrous, nice and slow. See the main cuts diagrams (pages 40–41). Each of these is then broken up into sub-cuts and all of those have different varieties of butchery and presentation within them too. However, generally, the main cuts can be put into three cooking categories:

Dry, which means it should be fried on its own, or with just a little bit of oil, and roasted without any need to be covered/steamed/braised. **Wet**, which basically needs us to help maintain or add to the moisture to prolong the cooking time, so that the connective tissue and fibres have enough time to break down (wet cooking keeps the moisture in, stopping the piece of meat from drying out). **Comminuted**, which means minced/ground and cubed beef. Often these are the same cuts as are used for 'wet', but the mincing/grinding and cubing breaks down the tissue and any sinew. (The burger developed as the 'poor man's steak' for the very reason that a cheaper source of beef was far more palatable if it was minced/ground to tenderize it and seasoned to give it more flavour. The same applies to meatloaf and meatballs for beef and sausages for pork.)

DRY-COOKING CUTS

The headline pieces and cuts, accounting for 90% of butchered steaks and joints, are covered here, but there might be other cuts available throughout the world, or other lesser-known and lesser-used pieces of beef. Ask your butcher for advice if you're unsure.

Sirloin (UK)/Short loin (US)

This is the strip of muscle along the top of the back; imagine where a saddle would go on a horse. It has a lovely coating of fat over the top (always look for light, cream fat, as darker fat means either a much older animal or, more commonly, grain- and cereal-fed), which gives it a lovely flavour for frying as steaks.

It makes a good roast, cut top to bottom to the length required and then rolled to thicken the mass of lean muscle underneath and keep it nice and juicy, while capping it with the fat to crisp under the roasting heat and release the juices into the meat. It can also be trimmed and broken down into various steaks and pieces. **Steaks** are best cut 2.5 cm/1 inch thick. In America, the **New York Strip Steak** is a thick-cut steak, often 5 cm/2 inches thick, from the leaner, higher end of the short loin. The **T-bone steak** and **porterhouse steak** are cut straight through the top end of the sirloin/short loin, including the connecting bone (a T-shape) and part of the fillet/tenderloin.

Stir-fry strips are often made from trimmed sirloin/short loin, because it's so lean and stir-frying needs only a short cooking time.

Rump (UK)/Sirloin (US)

The chunk of meat between the sirloin/short loin and the topside/round has various names depending on where you are in the world. In the UK, what is known as the rump is called the sirloin in the US, and then sub-divided into the top sirloin (used for roasting, grillling and stir-frying) and the tri-tip (which is grilled, roasted or slowly cooked). It can be trimmed and broken down into various cuts.

CUTS OF BEEF

Beef is butchered into slightly different cuts in different countries, and each cut can have various names. If in doubt, ask your butcher, as he or she will be familiar with the varied names of pieces of meat and which part of the animal they come from.

BRITISH BEEF CUTS

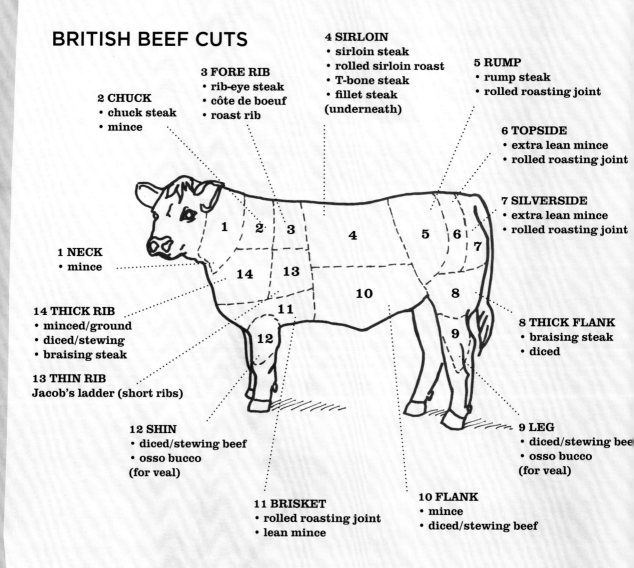

4 SIRLOIN
• sirloin steak
• rolled sirloin roast
• T-bone steak
• fillet steak
(underneath)

3 FORE RIB
• rib-eye steak
• côte de boeuf
• roast rib

5 RUMP
• rump steak
• rolled roasting joint

2 CHUCK
• chuck steak
• mince

6 TOPSIDE
• extra lean mince
• rolled roasting joint

7 SILVERSIDE
• extra lean mince
• rolled roasting joint

1 NECK
• mince

14 THICK RIB
• minced/ground
• diced/stewing
• braising steak

13 THIN RIB
Jacob's ladder (short ribs)

8 THICK FLANK
• braising steak
• diced

12 SHIN
• diced/stewing beef
• osso bucco
(for veal)

9 LEG
• diced/stewing beef
• osso bucco
(for veal)

11 BRISKET
• rolled roasting joint
• lean mince

10 FLANK
• mince
• diced/stewing beef

AMERICAN BEEF CUTS

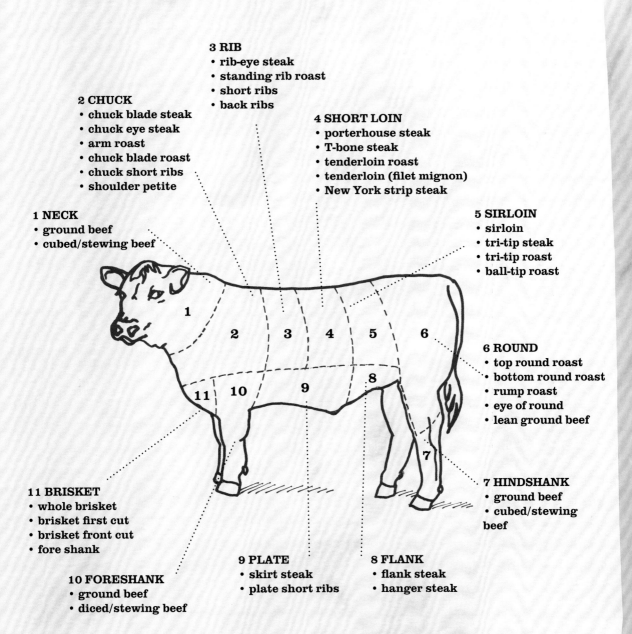

3 RIB
- rib-eye steak
- standing rib roast
- short ribs
- back ribs

2 CHUCK
- chuck blade steak
- chuck eye steak
- arm roast
- chuck blade roast
- chuck short ribs
- shoulder petite

4 SHORT LOIN
- porterhouse steak
- T-bone steak
- tenderloin roast
- tenderloin (filet mignon)
- New York strip steak

1 NECK
- ground beef
- cubed/stewing beef

5 SIRLOIN
- sirloin
- tri-tip steak
- tri-tip roast
- ball-tip roast

6 ROUND
- top round roast
- bottom round roast
- rump roast
- eye of round
- lean ground beef

7 HINDSHANK
- ground beef
- cubed/stewing beef

11 BRISKET
- whole brisket
- brisket first cut
- brisket front cut
- fore shank

9 PLATE
- skirt steak
- plate short ribs

8 FLANK
- flank steak
- hanger steak

10 FORESHANK
- ground beef
- diced/stewing beef

Steaks can vary in size from 225 g/8 oz. all the way up to 450 g/1 lb., as the cut is wide, so you can make a very large steak without having to cut too thick. **Rolled rump** is a roasting joint and it can be cut to your preferred size. It's best to use the top of the rump with the fat covering for the roasting and roll with twine. It's still fine for open roasting, but it's happier on a slightly lower heat for longer. **Cubed pieces** make fantastic stir-fries and pies. They're a little more expensive per kg/lb. so they're not used in mainstream restaurants, but if you want really good meat in, for example, Cornish Pasties (page 102), a rump/sirloin or round steak, cubed finely, is exceptional.

Fillet (UK)/Tenderloin (US)

This muscle runs along the sirloin and rump (UK) or short loin and sirloin (US) and does very little work. It is therefore the leanest and, because of this lack of fat and fibres through the meat, the most tender of steaks. It's so lean that it can be eaten raw as in Steak Tartare (page 137) or 'blue', which means barely cooked, just seared on the outside as in Beef Carpaccio (page 134). In other words, there is no connective tissue or fat to break down, so it's the quickest part to cook. Just be wary that, for this reason too, it can quite easily become dry, so I'd advise you to serve it cooked any more than medium to keep it succulent.

The whole fillet/tenderloin can be cooked whole as a quick or 'flash' roast (see page 153) or wrapped in pastry to make Beef Wellington (see page 154), or it can be broken down into various cuts. **Beef tournedos/filet mignon** comes from the tail end of the fillet/tenderloin, and can be roasted whole or cut into steaks. **Medallions** are square-cut steaks through the round, middle section. **Chateaubriand** is the 400–500 g/14 oz.–1 lb. of wider, uneven cut at the thick end of the piece, and is often cooked as one piece to share between two people.

Fore rib (UK)/Rib (US)

This is the muscle between the rib cage and spine, before the cavity for the lungs and organs begins. It's a lovely thick, rich cut of beef, with the best foundations for natural marbling (the fibres of fats that run through the meat) and perfect for roasting on the bone to add the extra conduction of heat and to release the juices from the marrow and reduced collagens that connect the to the bone. It's great for making delicious gravy.

The fore rib/rib can be trimmed and cut down into **rib-eye steaks**, which are about 2.5 cm/1 inch thick, boneless steaks. They are perfect for frying and griddling, and because there is a lot of fat running through the meat, it makes it almost impossible to overcook a well-farmed rib-eye steak. The longer you cook it, the more flavour will be released from the saturated fats, a short time and these will be chewy and fatty. **Rib on the bone** makes the ultimate roast in my opinion and can be cut to whichever size you require (roughly one rib bone for every 2–3 people). This is my favourite roasting meat and I go into more detail about prepping and roasting it on pages 45–47 and 199. **Côte de boeuf** is a trimmed, bone-in roast or thick rib steak – the rib-eye steak with the rib bone still attached.

WET-COOKING CUTS

These mid-priced cuts make up about 10% of our sales for pieces of meat. They tend to need more preparation or marinating, plus lower temperatures and higher moisture control.

Thin rib (UK)/Short rib (US)

Sometimes called 'Jacob's Ladder' in the UK, this is where the fore-rib is cut (basically to fit in a household oven!) and there is still very flavoursome meat between and over the outside of the bones. See page 171 for a slow-cooked Jacob's Ladder recipe.

Brisket (UK)/Brisket and plate (US)

Great for braising (see page 28), this is a flat piece of muscle on the underside of the animal. The section known as brisket in the UK includes the brisket and some of the plate in the US. This muscle does a lot of work and therefore requires long, slow cooking to tenderize it. It is popular as a rolled joint, so that the thin coating of fats is helpfully running through the middle. It is also often salted/brined to make salt beef/pastrami. **The hanger steak** or **onglet** is the muscle that works the diaphragm. The way it's used during the animal's life makes it very dark and bloody and it's not as tender as the prime cuts, but it's great for anyone who likes a rare piece of beef with a good bit of bite to it.

Topside (UK)/Top round (US) and Silverside (UK)/Bottom round (US)

The UK likes to separate the topside and silverside from the rump, but it's all part of the round in the US. It's very similar meat, but this far end, over the rear and down the back of the animal, is slightly leaner. These make great roasts if you braise or pot-roast them, covered, at a low temperature for a long period of time.

THE TRIM

And then we have the 'trim', which isn't a very flattering word, but it describes the rest of the body, which is still really good-quality, flavoursome meat. It's just that it's best for mincing and cubing. You'll sometimes hear it described by 'vl' (visual lean). This is an estimate of the share of fat in or on the meat so, for example, 95vl is very lean (like the topside/top round above) because that only leaves 5 per cent for fat. This lean grade is minced/ground and mixed with either fattier meat to balance it out or is used in recipes where you'd be cooking with butters or oils so aren't reliant on the natural fats present in the meat. A trim of 85vl is your reliable beef mince/ground beef that we use for burgers and meatballs, as it won't shrivel up and still has lots of flavour.

However, for **mincing/grinding**, I think the best cut is from the neck and shoulder, sometimes called 'chuck' or 'blade'. This tends to be about 85vl or 15% fat.

For **cubed or stewing meat**, shin/fore shank is terrific. If you imagine leg muscles and their role, you can see that there would need to be a lot of connective tissue. Thicker bits of sinew can be removed with a knife, but the collagen within and around the shin melts wonderfully in a slow-cooked casserole and turns to gelatine, naturally thickening your recipe.

OTHER CUTS

Ox cheek (UK)/beef cheek (US)

I'm not sure why the term 'ox' is still used in the UK for the cheek and tail; it's just beef. The ox is a working or 'draft' cattle and we don't use them for much work any more, but we still use the name for these. This is a dark, rich, sinewy cut – perfect for a slow-cooked casserole (see Ox Cheek and Blackberry Casserole, page 172).

Oxtail

This is, as the name suggests, the tail muscle. It is usually sliced widthways through the bone and it's great for a slow casserole/braise to break down all the connective tissue. It's also brilliant for making stock; you'll end up with a lovely, thick jelly stock, as the collagen will turn to gelatine and thicken it up naturally. Oxtail soup is a popular choice for chefs because the consistency basically looks after itself while it's simmering.

COOKTCHERY: RIB OF BEEF

This might just be my beef favouritism showing itself again, but this my favourite type of cooktchery to do and it looks very impressive. The bones are large and not as fiddly as lamb or pork, so you can really get stuck into it with knives to take off as much or as little as you'd like.

1. The 'chine' is the flat side of bone running from the corner where the ends of the ribs meet. We want to take this off whatever we do, as it's great for flavour but a pain when trying to carve. So get a knife underneath it and slice along to detach the bone from the meat. Wiggle a boning knife along the corner (**A**) to remove the piece completely – it's quite tough at the join of the ribs, so just be determined, it will come away. Remember not to worry if you leave a bit of meat on the bone, it doesn't matter.

2. Keep the chine to the side as we're going to use it for a roasting joint.

3. Then turn the rib on its end and, depending on which side of the animal it's from, you'll find a blade bone in the side of the piece. This is the end of the scapula. This might have already been taken out, but you'll see it and be able to feel it if it's there. Just slide a knife around the top and the bottom and twist it out.

4. Next we need to remove the nuchal ligament or 'paddywhack' (**B**). This is in all quadrupeds and basically, it helps hold the head up. It's almost pure protein, so would be very nutritious, but it's also like a big thick rubber band, and no amount of slow-cooking or tenderizing would make it good in terms of taste or to digest. However, dogs love it and it's the best natural dog chew – as the English nursery rhyme goes, 'Nick nack paddywhack, give a dog a bone, this old man came rolling home.' Just dry it for a couple of days to harden even more – leave it out on the side or in your fridge. It's not good for dogs if they swallow it, so keep it really dry so they're not tempted to swallow it whole (apologies to our friend, his dog and the results of the upset stomach from swallowing one whole...).

To get to the nuchal ligament, look again at the joint side on. Pointing towards where you started to cut the chine will be a thick yellowy piece, about 3 cm/1¼ inches wide (**C**). It runs all the way through, so you can't cut it out like the scapula; just pull back the top, or 'jacket', of the rib (use a knife to help) so that you can cut or pull out the paddywhack.

5. Now, if we're roasting, we might want to cut or saw through to make a smaller piece, or we might roast the whole piece. The smaller piece is called the 'fore rib' because it's at the fore end of the animal, not to be confused with a 'four rib' if it has four ribs on it... that's technically a fore four rib!

6. It's up to you if you want to trim the top of the bones. You don't have to, you can just cook it like this and it will be lovely. For a bit more presentation, cut down around the tops of the bones to expose about 2.5 cm/1 inch at the top. Scrape well so they're nice and clean after roasting. The meat you cut off is delicious and fatty and it's lovely in casseroles, so either keep it in the fridge for up to a week or pop it in the freezer for another time.

7. For roasting, though this isn't vital, you can now tie the 'chine' back onto the bottom (**D**). Like all cooking with the bone, the chine works as a natural heat conductor and helps the heat run through the main part ('eye') of the joint. It also helps to keep the moisture in by sealing this side of the beef. And it will help produce more

A

B

C

D

and richer liquids in the bottom of the roasting tray for if making gravy. You just put it back along the bottom and use the butcher's twine to tie it back on. Once the meat is roasted, just snip the strings and discard the chine so that the joint is easier to carve. Put the joint rib-side down and just carve from the top of the muscle.

8. If we're going to break the joint down some more or just use half of it for a roasting joint, we can remove the whole or half 'jacket' (**E**). There is a natural seam that you'll see with the fat through the meat where you can cut the top off. Essentially, it's the rib-eye joint still on the bone. This is 'côte de boeuf' and it's sometimes sold as trimmed joints, the width of two or more ribs, or it's sliced between the ribs for very large steaks (for two to share), which, as you can imagine, have all the juice and flavour of a rib-eye steak plus the moisture and the cooking benefits of having the rib still

attached. It's a terrific cut and looks impressive for entertaining, too.

9. To use the jacket, either dice or hand-mince (see page 27) for really flavoursome cuts or make a mini roast by folding it into a round bend and using the twine to cut it. It's such a terrific cut of meat that it's great to use it for something like this, and it's so juicy that dry-roasting even a small piece like this can't fail.

10. For the remaining part, we can now also remove the rib bones and slice just the centre meat into rib-eye steaks (**F**). The cut in the middle is, helpfully, already very even, so you just need to get equal widths for a perfect set of steaks, which will be ready to fry, griddle or cook on the barbecue/outdoor grill as you wish.

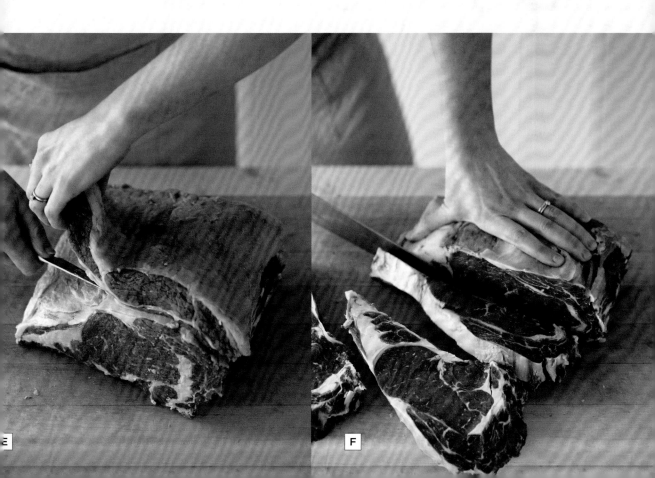

E

F

VEAL

Veal is an interesting subject. It's strange that we're comfortable eating lamb (more so than sheep's meat – mutton), but there is strong cultural concern about eating veal. Indeed, pigs, although fully grown because of their fast growth rate, tend to be younger than veal at slaughter. I agree with honouring an animal by eating it as late as you can, so that it has as long a life as possible and yields the most meat. However, there is a strong argument in favour of eating veal when reared well.

The main argument in favour of eating veal is when the breed of beef is for dairy. There are some dairy breeds that yield so little meat, even fully grown, that they can't be used for beef. However dairy cows are often mixed (or cross-bred) with some more muscular breeds. So in a dairy herd, if a bull calf is born to a dairy cow, it is going to be killed instantly, because there is no value in keeping the animal alive on a dairy farm. Is it better to rear the animal for a short time and sell it for veal?

Veal tends to be reared to 18–20 weeks. These are pretty big animals by now, weighing around 200 kg/550 lbs. – they look like small cows. In an ideal situation, the calves would remain with the mother and be milk-fed for this entire time. Unfortunately, the dairy farm is in a difficult position because their income is from the milk. So, not only are they rearing an animal that can't produce milk, they're assigning it the share of the milk they need to be getting from the mother as well. So, often, the calves are reared on formula, which is designed to have the nutrients for steady growth, like human baby milk formula.

In the UK, the RSPCA (the Royal Society of the Prevention of Cruelty to Animals) worked with farms (and dairy farms in particular) on the welfare and rearing of dairy calves. They designed the category, 'rose veal', which refers to the pink colour of the meat, which only occurs after a certain age (around 35 weeks).

Elsewhere in Europe, this meat is called 'young beef', another distinction from the young, white meat of veal.

So there are the principles of veal; the other question is the taste. What veal offers, which beef doesn't, is tenderness and very soluble fats and proteins, as well as very light (coloured and tasting) offal, such as heart and liver. Osso Bucco (page 156) for example, can't be made with the shin of beef, because the sinew around the bottom of the leg has been worked so much that it is very hard to break down, even with the slowest simmer, and the marrow has ossified and calcified. Veal bones and tissue don't add the strong dark 'beefy' taste to a stock either. The lean muscle, under 35 weeks, is a very light grey colour as the myoglobin still hasn't developed – another factor that makes the lean muscle very tender. Even rose veal, after 35 weeks, is only light pink.

The liver, kidney and heart are young and tender, in the same way that lamb's liver is infinitely more palatable than mutton liver, simply because it hasn't been used for as long.

LAMB AND MUTTON

The preference for lamb over mutton is similar in the UK, America and Western Europe and it's a very odd one. Meat is something that is so natural to us from an ancestral and evolutionary point of view, but it is also still something that challenges us.

I embrace the way we challenge our carnivorous practices and try to comprehend the ethics of killing and eating other living beings. On top of these individual questions, we are subjected to meat as an interminably 'hot' topic in the media... Meat is great for headlines, but this doesn't actually help us figure it out. You'd think it would encourage us to ask more questions, but it doesn't have that effect, not long term, because it sensationalizes it, fixates on the extremes and polarizes the argument so that the majority of the industry who fall between the extremes are either mislabelled and stereotyped or overlooked completely. That we eat mainly lamb rather than mutton in the UK and America is simply because mutton stopped being 'cool'.

Lamb and mutton in the UK

Lamb is more popular in the UK and Europe than it is in America. Before we began using synthetic materials, there was a booming wool trade in the UK in the mid-19th century. If a sheep got larger and older, you got more wool, so the bigger the better from the fleece point of view. Mutton was enjoyed as a welcome by-product. Cows at the time were very often 'draft' or working cattle, used for ploughing and harvesting. They were solid and muscular and therefore a bit chewy. Sheep weren't required to do anything but grow nice big fleeces of valuable wool.

In the early twentieth century the wool industry slowly started to diminish due to the development of synthetic materials and moving manufacturing abroad for cheaper production. At the same time, the two world wars had a big effect on rations. The infrastructure and supply set up for the (now greatly reduced) wool trade meant that there were a lot of sheep. There was therefore more mutton available for rations and this devalued it socially.

Following that, the increasing immigrant population from Arab states, the Caribbean and North Africa (and their religious traditions) arrived with mutton recipes, and it was further dissociated with 'traditional' Britain. However, it's a fantastic meat. It's got a little more fat, but the chops and loin are just as tender as lamb and I tend to slow-cook or braise a lot of lamb anyway, so why wouldn't I use mutton? It's cheaper, despite needing to be farmed for longer and not yielding much more meat, given that lamb is still 'lamb' up to 1 year old.

However, lamb is the big seller, so it is lamb we will celebrate in this collection of meat recipes, although I would happily have a go at all the lamb recipes with mutton, with the slightest reduction in temperature and the slightest increase in time.

Lamb and mutton in the US

Lamb was brought to the US by Spanish soldiers in the 16th century. Although lamb is easy to buy in the US, it has never become as popular here as it is in the UK and Europe, and the terms 'mutton' and 'hogget' (a sheep aged 12–18 months, between lamb and mutton) are more rarely used.

CUTS OF LAMB

Although there are not as many variations as with beef, lamb is butchered into slightly different cuts in different countries, and each cut can have slightly different names. If in doubt, ask your butcher.

BRITISH LAMB CUTS

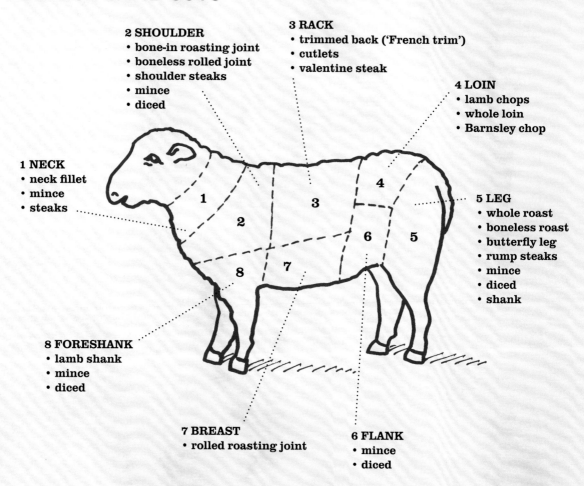

2 SHOULDER
- bone-in roasting joint
- boneless rolled joint
- shoulder steaks
- mince
- diced

3 RACK
- trimmed back ('French trim')
- cutlets
- valentine steak

4 LOIN
- lamb chops
- whole loin
- Barnsley chop

1 NECK
- neck fillet
- mince
- steaks

5 LEG
- whole roast
- boneless roast
- butterfly leg
- rump steaks
- mince
- diced
- shank

8 FORESHANK
- lamb shank
- mince
- diced

7 BREAST
- rolled roasting joint

6 FLANK
- mince
- diced

AMERICAN LAMB CUTS

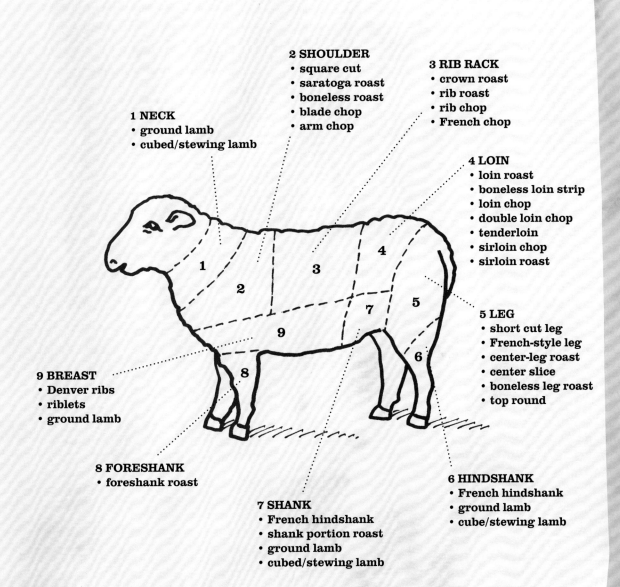

2 SHOULDER
- square cut
- saratoga roast
- boneless roast
- blade chop
- arm chop

3 RIB RACK
- crown roast
- rib roast
- rib chop
- French chop

1 NECK
- ground lamb
- cubed/stewing lamb

4 LOIN
- loin roast
- boneless loin strip
- loin chop
- double loin chop
- tenderloin
- sirloin chop
- sirloin roast

5 LEG
- short cut leg
- French-style leg
- center-leg roast
- center slice
- boneless leg roast
- top round

9 BREAST
- Denver ribs
- riblets
- ground lamb

8 FORESHANK
- foreshank roast

7 SHANK
- French hindshank
- shank portion roast
- ground lamb
- cubed/stewing lamb

6 HINDSHANK
- French hindshank
- ground lamb
- cube/stewing lamb

UNDERSTANDING LAMB CUTS

A 'spring lamb' is under three months old and the most tender. Again, like veal, they grow faster than you'd imagine and already look quite sheep-like at this stage. Most lamb is slaughtered around 5–6 months old, to yield more meat. Up to 1 year old it is 'lamb'; for its second year, it's called 'hogget', and then, from its second summer, it's called 'mutton'. A lot of the cuts and cooking methods are the same as for beef, it's just smaller and, as I discovered, a bit more fiddly!

DRY-COOKING CUTS
Rump (UK)/Round (US)
On the shape of a lamb, this is the top of the leg. It is also sometimes called the 'chump' in the UK or sirloin in the US. This can be sliced as steaks (see opposite) or rolled into a small roast.

Loin
This is often trimmed of all bone and sinew and sold as fillet or loin, or cleavered between the thin ribs/vertebrae and sold as loin chops. There is a small fillet/tenderloin too.

Rack
This is the rib section. This is often French trimmed/Frenched to clean along the top, which looks impressive, yields very tender and juicy meat, it doesn't take very long to roast. The rack, with smaller bones than the loin chop end, can be cut down the middle, between the bones to create **cutlets or rib/rack chops**, ideal for grilling/broiling or cooking in griddle pans.

Leg
Ideal for a large bone-in roast or butterflied to remove the bone. (See pages 53–54.)

WET-COOKING CUTS
Shank
This is the muscle around the front or hind leg with the hoof removed. It is best slow-cooked, as it has a lot of connective tissue.

Shoulder
Some recipes just remove the top end of the ribs and keep both shoulder bones and the scapula, but often the bones and scapula are removed, the front shank tunnel-boned and the muscle trimmed and rolled for a slow-roasting joint, ideal for braising or pot-roasting. In the US, it is more likely that the shoulder includes the scrag but not any part of the shank.

Breast
This is a thin strip of meat, which is cut off the breast bone, trimmed and rolled. It benefits from even slower and lower time and temperature.

Neck and scrag end (UK)/upper shoulder (US)
Great for mincing/grinding for burgers, meatballs or sausages.

OTHER BITS
Offal (UK)/variety meats (US)
The **'pluck'** (**kidney, liver, heart** and **lungs/ lights**) are tender and have a lighter taste than grown sheep. Ideal for Homemade Haggis (page 98) if they are available. **Intestines** are used for natural casings for non-pork sausages.

Bones
The marrow and connective tissue from lamb are ideal for making stock, as the viscosity from the collagen naturally thickens to a jellied stock or as the base for a delicious casserole.

COOKTCHERY: LEG OF LAMB

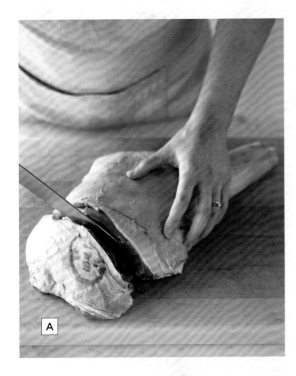

A

Doing your own cooktchery more than halves the cost of buying a lot of the lamb leg pieces pre-cut. It's all surprisingly easy to do when you don't have to do it the 'right' way, in terms of what constitutes butchery. Just ask yourself the simple question, does this bit look like I want to eat it? If not, cut it out. To start with, please begin with a clean surface, give it a really good wash down with very hot water and cleaning liquids – the same for the chopping board, knives and your hands, of course.

1. Ask for a whole leg of lamb with the rump/round still attached to the top to get the most out of this. (If you have bought a meat saw, ask for the shank to be on, even the hoof too, as you can remove that if you like.)

2. Your fingers are your best guide for removing the bits that don't cook well or taste nice. Bone, obviously, is easy to detect, but also connective tissues and ligaments that are hard to break down. It's easiest to push your fingers into the meat and if these bits resist or feel thick and tough, like elastic bands or string, then you'll know to cut them out, particularly if you're not slow-cooking the meat.

3. Lay the leg, inside facing up, so that the fat coating is flat on the chopping board. In line with the top of the hip bone, maybe a little bit before the end of the bone if you can get the knife in, slice clean through to take all of the top muscle off (**A**).

4. This top muscle can be rolled with twine to make a small roasting joint or sliced into steaks. You'll see a small grey sphere among the meat, which is a gland. Cut it out. Incidentally, if you slice this through the middle, check the colour – it's a good indication of the quality and age of the lamb. It should be a very light grey – if it's dark grey or brown-grey, then it's an older lamb and possibly not in the best health. The meat will likely still be fine, just give it a good sniff to check that it doesn't smell off or 'tainted' and perhaps choose a recipe with a good bit of marinating to balance the flavour, rather than the traditional dry roast. The top muscle can also be sliced into rump/round steaks. Lovely for pan-frying in a frying pan/skillet or popping on the barbecue/outdoor grill.

5. Below that, you have the main leg of lamb, great for a Classic Roast Leg of Lamb (page 188) but there's still more you can do with it too...

6. If you have a saw, you can make a lamb shank. Feel where the bulge in the muscle has a small ridge, approximately 12 cm/5 inches above the start of the muscle on the leg bone. Use your knife to cut through the meat and around the bone, and then use your meat saw to cut through the bone to detach it. Stand the triangular piece of meat on its end and use your paring knife to slice the thin end of meat away from the bone; keep it attached but bring it a little off the bone and scrape the bone clean. This is just a presentation thing so that the bone looks very clean after cooking and the connective tissue at the end there has some help breaking down during cooking too.

7. On the outside of the leg, cut off any thick or very hard bits of fat from the surface or from around the edges of the leg. The white, crumbling fat will dissolve when you cook it but any larger bits will be better to be cut off.

8. For a boneless leg joint, you can happily keep the shank on or off. The whole leg bone can be tunnel-boned (see page 27) but it's easier to slice it out and then either roll the joint or butterfly it. Put the piece with the inside leg facing up again and, with the tip of your knife, slice into the meat tightly next to one side of the hip bone (**B**). Then bring the knife all the way down the one side of the bone so you make a clean cut through the middle of the meat. Come all the way down to the other end, if you like, as it's easier. Don't be afraid to angle the tip of the knife into the bone to make sure that you're staying nice and close to it; you probably won't take a chip off the bone but, if it's a young ('spring') lamb, or you have a very well-sharpened knife, you might take a bit off. But we're going to trim the inside of the meat anyway, so you'll soon see the small, flat white disc of hard bone attached to the meat and know to cut it out.

Use your fingers to pull back the meat to give some tension, then you can keep using your paring knife to cut close to the top of the bone and then, very simply down the other side and under the bottom, just by pulling the meat (**C**) gently away from the bone to get some tension and putting the sharp, thin tip of the paring knife into the meat to slice it (**D**).

9. Now you have a boneless leg of lamb, just open out the meat, use your fingers to squeeze the surface and cut out anything hard or stringy. Just leave all the lovely, rich, dark, lean meat where it is.

10. Then to butterfly it, imagine that you're trying to cover as much of the chopping board with a single piece as possible. You basically angle the knife parallel to the board and slice in sideways to halve the depth of the lamb meat and then fold that piece out to increase the surface size of the joint, like a flat butterfly (**E**). You can then, if it's still thick, do the same to that piece to fold it out in another angle. This is great for chucking on the barbecue/outdoor grill or under the grill/broiler and lovely with a marinade too.

11. You can also butterfly-cut it for the benefit of marinating (so that the flavours and acids reach much further into the meat) and then roll it, following the instructions on page 26.

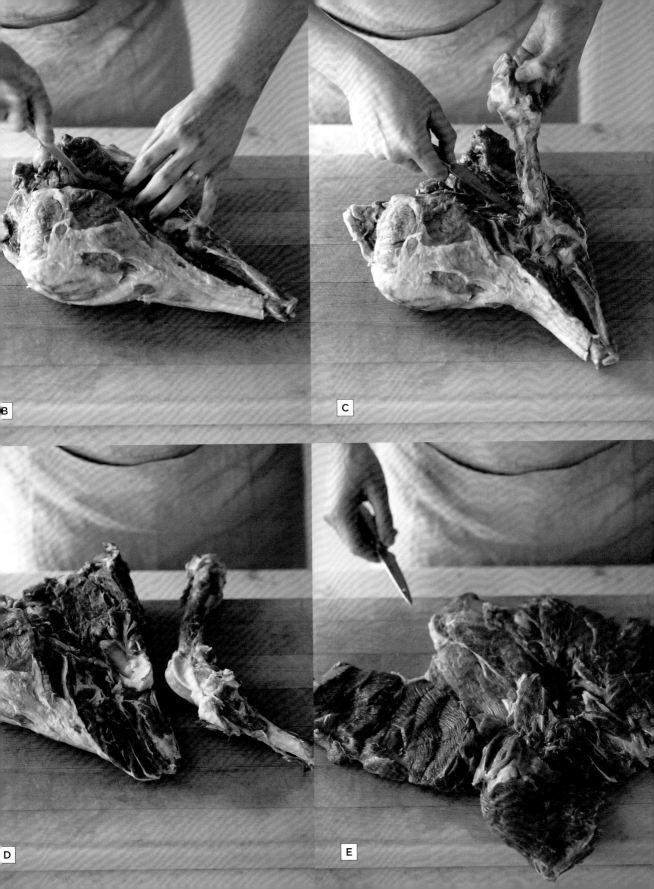

PORK

Pork is a fascinating meat to study, both in terms of taste and principles. Pork gives the widest range of taste and recipes once you take into account not just the raw meat cuts, listed below, but the popularity of minced/ground products (such as sausages), semi-cured or brined products (such as bacon), and fully cured products (known as charcuterie) to which the pig lends far more varieties and traditions than any other meat. For the same reason that pork dominates the popular cured-meat products, it is (along with chicken) the most consumed meat on average around the world. This is because they can be farmed so fast... not necessarily 'fast' as in 'cheap' or unethical, but pigs breed and grow at an astonishing rate.

Even a slow, traditional, 'free-range' pig farm can produce 2.2 rounds (or generations) of pigs in a year. The impregnating and gestation is often described as 'three months, three weeks, three days'. The piglets wean (even unaided) far quicker than other animals and their growth rate to 'full-grown' (i.e., when there is no further commercial value to keep finishing them) is under 5 months. Indeed, a lot of breeds (developed for just this sort of rate) are 'finished' in under 14 weeks.

Incidentally, this provides an interesting angle on the controversy around the age of an animal when it's killed – what constitutes a full life when pigs are technically still within the 'milk-fed veal' age or the 'spring lamb' age. 'Suckling pig' is even younger – around 4–6 weeks old.

On top of this fantastic productivity, they have big litters; 6–12 piglets at a time! Compared to singles, twins and (very occasionally) triplets in sheep and cows.

Cured pork

Because of this availability, our palates and our processes with pork are more advanced, especially with curing meats. We borrow the French word 'charcuterie', which comes from the 'charcutier' or the 'pig butcher'. The range of pig products was so vast that the 'boucher' (butcher) took all other meats, and the 'charcutier' took the pig products. Curing meats was man's battle against bacteria, and our friends in Italy, France and Spain were leagues ahead in developing salami, saucisson and chorizo respectively.

On top of all the fully cured meats, we eat a vast amount bacon and ham.

Pork principles

There are religious considerations for pork, as it is not permitted by the laws of Islam and Judaism. However, pork is extremely popular in China, America, the UK and Europe.

From a principles point of view, I feel that pork challenges the conscience more than any other meat. Having spoken to other people in farming and slaughter, I'm not alone in detecting far more 'thought' in pigs than any other animal. I describe this now only to further examine the accountability and responsibility of a modern meat supply.

If you look a cow or sheep in the eye, it doesn't look back. Humans begin interpreting non-verbal communication and signals from a surprisingly young age, just a few weeks, in fact. We are genetically and instinctively programmed to read faces and communicate with other humans. A cow or sheep will look straight past you. If they happen to make eye contact, it is very little more than coincidence. There is very little searching in their look. A pig however... well, it was really a race to opposable thumbs with these ones, I reckon. They'll look right back at you, they can be trained and be taught their name (like a dog), they are happiest in groups like 'tribes', they have hierarchies within these groups like humans and apes, and they're carnivores like humans too; they'll eat anything... and when they look at you, you know that they're thinking this as well. In fact, I'm sure they'd have as many cuts, curing methods and make crackling out of us too, if we weren't as nimble.

The significance of this is the responsibility to witness slaughter. I had seen a lot of cattle and lambs slaughtered before I first saw a pig being slaughtered. I was surprised at what a different effect it had on me to stand on the live side and help lead the pigs to the stun (or gas and stun). As with all good abattoirs/slaughterhouses, the pigs in the two systems that I have been to, the animals are calm, there is no rough handling by the staff and (for the benefit of the meat and the animals) the pigs are led in twos, so that they remain calm and there is less adrenalin released.

However, they all look at you before they go in, properly, I feel, look at you, and there is a searching in the eyes. If you are still happy with and confident in the abilities, practices and ethics of the abattoir/slaughterhouse and the slaughtermen after this, then you have found your supply (with, of course, the farm(s) you trust, too). It was one of the hardest challenges for me and I'm pleased to have done it, to have respected it and, most importantly, to be able to trust the abattoir/slaughterhouse.

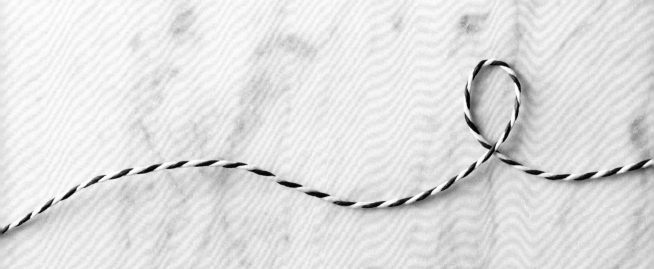

CUTS OF PORK

BRITISH PORK CUTS

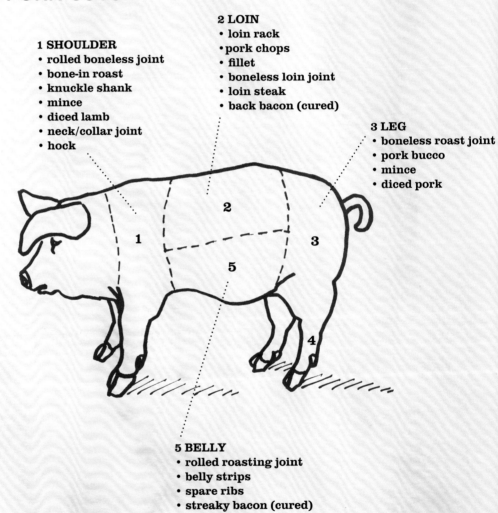

1 SHOULDER
- rolled boneless joint
- bone-in roast
- knuckle shank
- mince
- diced lamb
- neck/collar joint
- hock

2 LOIN
- loin rack
- pork chops
- fillet
- boneless loin joint
- loin steak
- back bacon (cured)

3 LEG
- boneless roast joint
- pork bucco
- mince
- diced pork

5 BELLY
- rolled roasting joint
- belly strips
- spare ribs
- streaky bacon (cured)

AMERICAN PORK CUTS

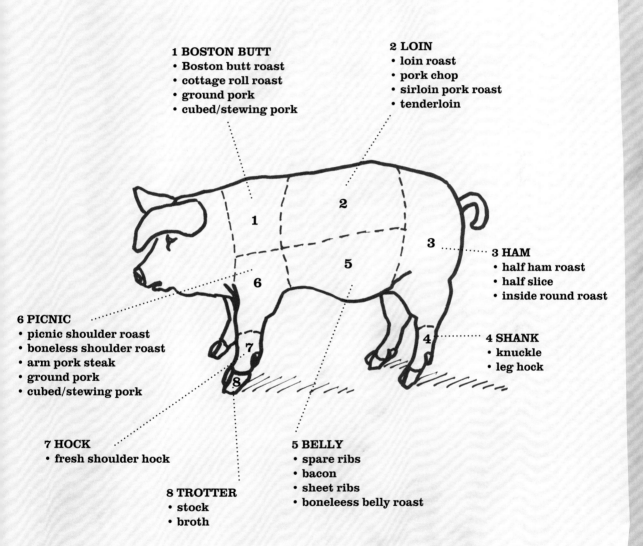

1 BOSTON BUTT
- Boston butt roast
- cottage roll roast
- ground pork
- cubed/stewing pork

2 LOIN
- loin roast
- pork chop
- sirloin pork roast
- tenderloin

3 HAM
- half ham roast
- half slice
- inside round roast

4 SHANK
- knuckle
- leg hock

6 PICNIC
- picnic shoulder roast
- boneless shoulder roast
- arm pork steak
- ground pork
- cubed/stewing pork

7 HOCK
- fresh shoulder hock

8 TROTTER
- stock
- broth

5 BELLY
- spare ribs
- bacon
- sheet ribs
- boneleess belly roast

UNDERSTANDING PORK CUTS

There are some cuts (like the Boston butt, used for pulled pork), which benefit from being covered when roasted but, generally, the high water content in the pork means that it's quite wet to begin with and all the cuts can be cooked using dry-cooking methods, such as roasting or grilling/broiling. For this same natural 'wetness' reason, pork doesn't hang well. It will tenderize, but its wetness is too productive for the growth of bacteria, so it is only chilled in the fridge for 2–4 days before cutting and packing.

DRY-COOKING CUTS
Shoulder
See the cooktchery feature (pages 61–62) for cutting the shoulder into boneless and bone-in roasting cuts, neck fillet, collar and shank. In the US, the shank is rarely considered part of the shoulder, which is instead divided into the Boston butt (used for pulled pork) and picnic cuts. For cured products, the shoulder is transformed into coppa.

Loin
Much like the sirloin in beef, this is the 'saddle' along the top of the pig. It can be a loin rack joint or cut into pork chops. It is very popular cured for bacon (known as 'back bacon' in its uncooked form the UK and, when cooked, 'Canadian bacon' in the US).

Spare ribs
These lead down the side/belly, like short ribs in beef. These are sawn left to right (to remove the loin, above) and can be left whole or cut between the ribs so that there is a coating of the intercostal muscle around them.

Belly/Side
This is the long strip along the underside of the body. It is very versatile and can be roasted whole, rolled with butcher's twine (see page 26) and roasted, cut into slices (see Pork and Boston Beans, page 163) or diced for lardons. It's also very popular for bacon (known as 'streaky bacon' in the UK or 'fatty bacon' in the US).

The Leg
It's large, so the leg is usually portioned into boneless rolled roasting joints, rather than being sold whole. Along the top, from inside, is the fillet/tenderloin for roasting whole or cutting into steaks/medallions. Also leg steaks, similar to rump/round. The leg is famous for bone-in curing, such as gammon/bone-in ham, Parma Ham and Jamón Ibérico, and boneless for general prosciutto and ham.

WET-COOKING CUTS
Pig cheek, like ox/beef cheek, is more fibrous, but makes great cubed pork for casseroles and slower cooks.

OFFAL (UK)/VARIETY MEATS (US)
The **'pluck'** or **heart**, **lung**, **liver** and **kidneys** can be used for faggots (like the recipe on page 87), if you can get hold of them in your country.

Trotters can be stripped for mincing/grinding and cubed or boiled for stock.

COOKTCHERY: PORK SHOULDER

This follows similar fundamentals to the leg of lamb, basically cutting out the bones and then using the pieces separately. Again, buying the whole piece tends to work out at less than half the price per kg/lb. on average than buying the cut pieces. Remember that a pork shoulder is very big – three times the size of a leg of lamb, for example, so make sure you have a big gathering or enough room in your freezer to make use of all that you cut down.

You can request for the trotter to be removed first or just use a meat saw to take it off.

Pigs have skin (or 'rind'), unlike cows that have a hide, so this is why there is rind on the pork and, with some scoring, salt and high heat, we'll get crackling too. If you'd prefer not to have crackling and would just like the coating of light fat underneath, then just use a sharp knife to take if off in strips from around the whole shoulder. This is easier done at this stage (or order a rindless whole shoulder to make it even easier) and though there are some skills for removing the rind, they are a bit fiddly, so just keep cutting it off in strips with a chef's knife (or a paring knife first to get between the rind and the skin) until it's all off.

If you're keeping the rind on, always score diagonal lines across it. This helps release the juices from the fat below as well as (for crackling) penetrating the surface with salt to dehydrate the fats underneath and make it dissolve and harden.

1. You'll probably still have the top of the rib cage attached – skip to the next point if you don't. For this, as with all cooktchery, it's common sense – you want to get the bones off. I tend to hold it up on its 'end' so that the top of the ribs is towards me. Then I use a paring knife (or boning knife) to wiggle under the flat bones and tightly underneath them (be careful not to take too much off the collar joint beneath them, as this is lovely pork) and then up, under

and around the inside of the ribs. You can score a line down each side of the ribs first to try and keep the intercostal muscles attached as well but, again, you're not a commercial operation and the difference of this tiny bit of meat from in between the bones isn't going to make much difference. So keep wiggling along the bones until that plate of ribs comes off completely. You can use this for broth, although there isn't a lot of marrow in these thin bones, so a stock won't quite have the flavour or the thickness.

2. You have three bones and an elbow to deal with. I'd recommend removing the main leg bone (radius) from the top first. This piece of meat is best for a slow bone-in roast or pulled pork. With the rind facing up, feel and look for a natural curve at the base of the leg. There's usually a ridge, a natural dip in the muscle formation (**A**). Just use a big knife to cut that end off; you might need to feel for the end of the central bone to be able to cut through the connecting socket (**B**). Score the rind and use for Pulled Pork Shoulder with BBQ Sauce (see page 164) or a roasting joint.

3. Keeping the rind facing down, feel for the remaining bones. The humerus comes away from the elbow, back through the shoulder. Use your paring (or boning) knife to cut along one side of the bone. Once you've done one side, you'll be able to see the bone at the top and prise away the meat with the tip of your knife. Cut underneath it to remove the bone fully.

Don't worry that the meat is opening out – you're going to roll it anyway and now we want to get to the connective tissue to cut out any thicker bits of sinew, so just feel for any tough strains or silvery sinews.

4. Once that bone is out (which looks most like a classic dog bone if you have a willing dog waiting patiently!), you'll be able to feel where the top of it was to find the scapula (the shoulder blade bone, which looks like a triangle (**C**)). This has a deceptively knobbly top to it because of the elbow, so you need to wiggle the knife in and around the top with a good bit of confidence. Slice down one side and then use the sharp tip of the knife to cut the lean muscle away from the top of the bone. Cut through the connective tendon that attaches the top to the radius. Then scrape under the scapula a little and you'll see that the top end has come away from the meat. You can either get a good grip and pull this towards you to pull it out, or you can just keep using the sharp tip of your paring knife to cut it out. Discard the bone.

5. You now have a big expanse of meat. Use your eyes and your fingers to cut out as much of the non-pink, non-meaty looking tissue. Remember that you're going to roll it so try not to cut through the rind, but otherwise don't worry about the appearance of the underside of the meat (**D**).

6. You have a neck joint along the top. Depending on how far back the shoulder was cut will determine how much of this piece you'll get. You'll find the neck joint along the top of the piece, with natural lines to show where to cut it. You can roast this as a piece, 'bard' it with some fat from elsewhere on the shoulder, or you can cut it into steaks. It's also used to make coppa, a delicious cured meat (**E**).

7. With the remaining shoulder piece, you can either cube or mince/grind it for casseroles, pork burgers, sausages, etc., or roll it into one very large or two small shoulder joints. You can weigh the whole piece to get an idea of what you're dealing with – 225 g/8 oz. per person is a good serving suggestion, so you can cut it to the size you need (**F**). if your kitchen scales don't go above a very high weight, just put some greaseproof paper or something on your bathroom scales, or weigh yourself holding the joint and subtract your weight without!

8. You can roll the joints with separate ties (see page 26 on rolling) and score the rind to help make crackling (**G** and **H**).

9. You can also butterfly the shoulder like we did with the leg of lamb (see page 54) to produce more surface area for a marinade or stuffed joint recipe (see Stuffed Rolled Pork Shoulder on page 187).

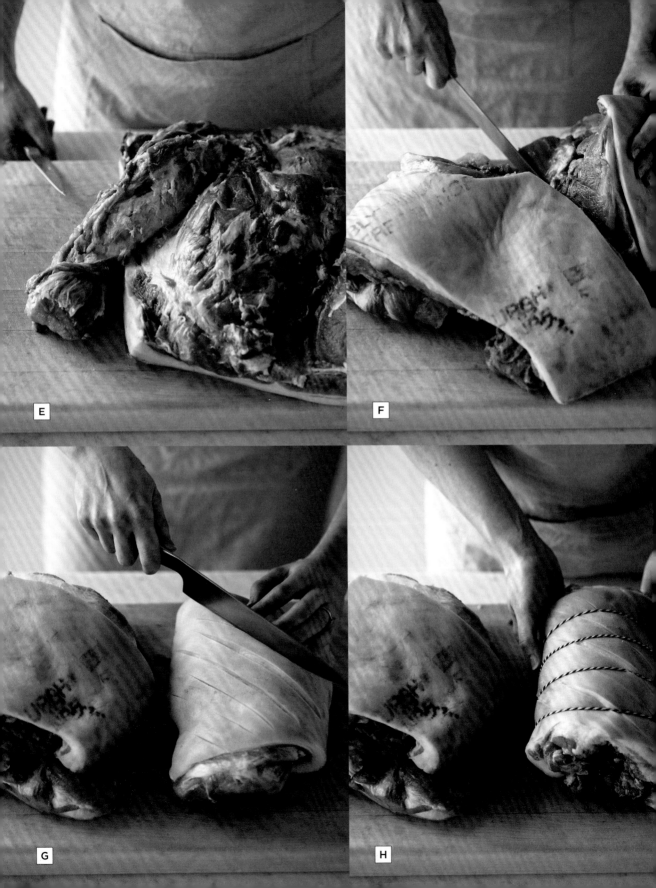

CHICKEN AND POULTRY

Chicken is by far the most popular and common member of the poultry family, and it is consumed more than any other meat. Like the pig, it breeds extremely efficiently and grows to full size in 6 weeks in a fairly intensive system or 18–20 weeks for a slow-farmed free-range chicken.

Chicken's popularity is the bird's downfall. The market for it is huge, so the competition is high and the race to be the cheapest has come entirely at the cost to the bird's quality of life. The popularity of the meat, and possibly because we're more detached from birds than other mammals, with whom we share certain qualities, means that some of the worst cases of ill treatment occur in poor chicken farming. As ever, the cost to principles is undeniably reflected in the taste too. If you roast a well-farmed chicken in the same oven as an intensively farmed chicken for the same amount of time and with the same amount of care, preparation and basting, you will end up with two very different pieces of meat. Though, as I mentioned, it is impossible to define tastes as 'better', one can definitely identify what is superior and a dry, shrivelled, chewy chicken is vastly inferior to a luscious, succulent, flavourful one that hasn't shrunk to a third of its raw size. Fast-farmed chicken will leave you with little meat and even less flavour.

Health and safety
Chicken is a headliner for health and hygiene risks. The meat, in fact, is no more susceptible to bacteria than other animals, but the nature of the mass slaughter and handling makes for a higher-risk product. There is some 'dry-plucking' but it's an expensive, labour-intensive method, so usually the birds are clamped onto a rail after gassing (you couldn't stun a chicken because you wouldn't be able to hold it place and the head is too small) and then flushed with jets of water to help the pluckers remove the feathers. The high levels of water combined with the warm body of the bird make it a perfect place for bacteria, plus the plucking leaves punctures in the skin for these to hide. The 'drawing' (or gutting) has to happen very fast for the volume of birds coming through even a high-level killing floor, so there is a risk of fecal contamination as well.

Types of chicken
In the category of chickens, there are many varietes of bird. **Poussins** are very young chickens (4–6 weeks old, or 'double poussins' are 6–12 weeks old). **Spring chicken** is 10–12 weeks old. **Roasting chicken** (usually just called 'whole chicken') is generally around 3 months. The better farmed, the more plump. Free-range chickens will be 1.4–2.2 kg/3–5 lbs. Capon (a castrated cockerel) can be up to 4 kg/8½ lbs. Not as popular any more, capon is quite tough, so a slower roasting, like a goose, is better.

Free range
Well-farmed chicken will be 'free-range', in other words, free to walk around. They choose to go under cover, even if not ushered, for night, as do pigs. They will peck at the ground and eat clover and pasture and often have troughs of corn undercover to top up their feed as they wish. A good chicken is usually large and plump and can be cut down to be used for lots of meals (see pages 69–71).

Duck

A naturally more fatty bird, with proportionally less edible muscle. A 1.8 kg/4 lbs. chicken will serve 4–5 people, whereas the same weight duck will go around 2–3 people and there isn't much use serving the thighs or legs separately, unless you add multiple accompaniments. The breasts are delicious though, with more flavour and almost as much meat as chicken. Great cubed as well: see Duck, Venison and Halloumi skewers (page 140).

Goose

Goose used to be more popular than turkey at Christmas in the UK, whereas the trend has definitely moved to turkey. Quite like duck, it's a lot of fat and bone to not as much muscle, which is probably why turkey has taken over. See the recipe for Roast Goose, page 205. The strained fats from cooking a goose or a duck make a very thick, flavoursome cooking fat, a real treat for perfect roast potatoes.

Turkey

The traditional Thanksgiving meal, turkey is popular in the UK, as well as America now. The meat is very lean, often recommended for low-fat/high-protein diets. For a classic holiday roast, see page 212.

Cooking poultry

The lean meat can benefit from the 'bard' method of wrapping bacon or pork fats over the top for roasting. Similarly, minced/ground chicken and turkey often have minced pork fat in them to prevent shrivelling and drying when cooked. (Check the ingredients on minced/ground poultry products to avoid other meats or added fats.)

Poaching is great for rolled and stuffed chicken or for keeping the tenderness on a lower temperature. Steamed chicken is popular for people following extremely-low fat diets.

POULTRY CUTS
Whole bird

Great for roasting whole (with some basting, particularly for turkey) or boned out (see pages 69–71) and stuffed (see Poached Whole Ballotine Chicken with Basil Pesto, page 139).

Crown/whole breast

This is the name for the breast joints on the bone but with the back bone, legs/thighs (and sometimes wings) removed. It's most popular with turkey because it makes a much smaller joint, but still has the moisture and juices from the bones. It's ideal for making gravy.

Breast fillets/boneless breasts

Birds are totally different from mammals in that they carry their muscles on the front (because of their wings). Breast fillets are cut off the rib cage and are great for roasting or stuffing and coating.

Legs

Legs can subsequently be jointed into thighs and drumsticks. This meat is darker and a bit richer, making it great for casseroles, such as Coq au Vin (page 160) on the bone. You can also use them boneless (see page 70 for how to do this).

Wings

Often marinated and cooked on the barbecue/outdoor grill or in a griddle pan. The meat is very succulent and has lots of flavour, but they're fiddly – best for picking up and nibbling.

OTHER BITS
Liver

Chicken liver is popular as it has a light flavour and fries well. It is most popular for pâtés (see Chicken Liver Pâté, page 127).

Bones

The carcass is great for making delicious stock and nutritious broth (see page 32).

COOKTCHERY: CHICKEN BREAKDOWN

Chicken is the meat that tragically boasts some of the worst examples of criminal animal-rearing. People ask why good chicken is so expensive but they don't ask why cheap chicken is so cheap. A good chicken is usually large and plump and can be used for lots of meals, so here's a way to make the most of it. It's always better value to buy a whole chicken and break it down into portions yourself. If you buy butchered breasts and thighs, you understandably pay for the cost of the cutting, packaging, transportation, space on the shelf and labour.

1. Start with the whole chicken, plucked and drawn. Remove any remaining entrails and giblets inside but nearly all trade in chickens is for fully eviscerated birds.

2. Take off any holding ties around the legs or wings too. These are just used to hold its shape for presentation as well as ease of getting it into any packaging.

3. With the breast side up, pull one of the legs away from the body to make the skin more taut and, with a sharp knife, cut towards the body through the middle of the skin that attaches it (**A**).

4. Then carry on with the knife around the very base of the leg, alongside the bone of the body, as close as you can (**B**). You want a funnel

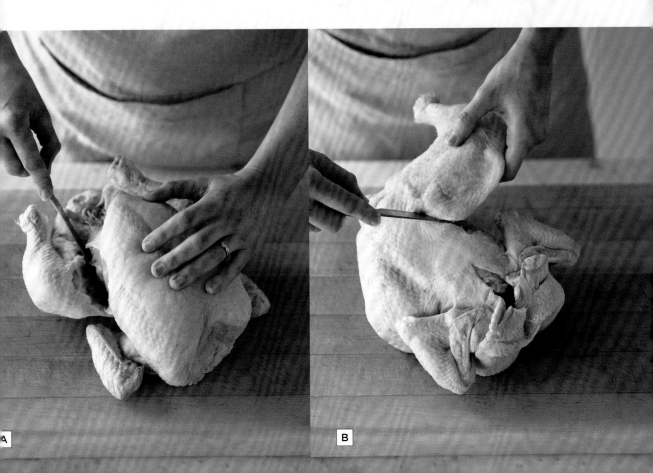

A B

shape at the top of the thigh so that you haven't left too much chicken on the bone on this side because it's not attached to another piece of muscle so you want to keep it attached to the thigh.

5. When you've cut all around, it's just the hip bone attached – bend it back/away from you to crack it and then you'll be able to use the knife to cut through the cartilage in the middle. You can then cut around the joint in the middle to detach the thigh and drumstick in the same way. Set them aside for now

6. Then the breasts. The smaller and sharper the knife, the better (a paring knife), and remember that it's really just the end bit you want to work with. Little 'nicks' are better than deep slices, which might result in you cutting a piece off that you can't see from the surface and you can't reattach. Start along the top, straight down the middle (**C**) and try and cut along the ridge of the bone, either start just to the left or just to the right. Angle the knife as you come around and take your time so that you try not to leave any meat on the carcass. These boneless breasts retail for, on average, three times the price per kg/lb. than a whole chicken.

7. Cut off the wings, just clean through the joint – pull the wing away from the body to create the tension (**D**). Great in stock or marinated and cooked on the barbecue/outdoor grill. Do the same on the other side.

8. Take the thigh, cut around with the knife, snap the bone (**E**), snip the attaching tendons and separate. Now you have a bone-in thigh and a drumstick – perfect for cooking on the barbecue/outdoor grill or putting in casseroles.

9. You can lay the thigh skin-side down and cut out the bone to make a boneless thigh too. Just run the knife along the sides of the bone and cut it out, then remove anything that looks 'sinewy' – basically, let your instincts take over. If it looks like it'll be chewy and hard to digest, cut it out. Lean muscle looks totally simple to us.

This boneless thigh that you've made in about 5 minutes would retail at double the price you paid for it attached to the whole chicken.

10. Do the same to the other side so that you have two sets of thighs and drumsticks to go with the wings you've already removed (**F**). (You can take the meat off the drumsticks, but you're working with three different muscles and some fiddly bones and tendons. Better to use the drumstick for the barbecue/outdoor grill or cooking whole in casseroles or roasts, then you can take the meat off the bone once cooked, as it falls off easily.)

11. Use the carcass to make lovely chicken stock (see page 32).

12. Tightly wrap the parts you're not using straight away to keep in your fridge (for up to the use-by date stated on the whole chicken) or pop in the freezer for up to 3 months.

13. To make a boneless whole chicken, start with a pair of scissors to cut just to the left or right of the breast bone. Then switch to a knife to cut out all the bones – don't worry too much about the order, just be careful not to nick the skin because that, particularly around the legs, is what's going to hold it together so you can stuff and roll it. The wings are too small to bone out, and if you cut them off, you make two large holes in the bird, so I just leave them where they are and then cut them off after. It's fiddly, but there's no wrong way if you just take each section at a time and remove all the bone. For the back plate, turn the bird carefully over and slide a knife in, just a little at a time to cut the skin away from the bone. You'll find a knack that works for you.

GAME

The term 'game' refers to wild animals, killed either for sport or breeding control (known as culling) and then eaten. There are mammals and poultry under this category, the most popular of which I will cover here, although there may be other popular or more unusual local game meats in your area. Ask your butcher for seasonal recommendations.

Both types of game will usually be hung for at least a couple of weeks. Feather game will be hung with the feathers still unplucked to extend the life (meaning there is less access for bacteria and less water in the handling to encourage the multiplying of bacteria on the skin).

There's a strong 'gamey' flavour to this meat and it's not for everyone. The recipes to cook with it often include marinating in some degree of acidity (vinegars or citric juices) to help break down that strong flavour as well as tenderize the meat by dissolving some of the proteins.

MAMMALS (AKA FUR GAME)
Deer (venison)
Roebuck
Wild boar
Rabbit
Hare

BIRDS (AKA FEATHER GAME)
Guinea fowl
Partridge
Pigeon
Grouse
Pheasant
Quail
Wild duck
Woodcock

Fur game

These animals are very lean. They are more active than domestic livestock and burn a lot of calories. 'Barding' (coating with fats, see page 30) is popular for these meats, as is mixing them into recipes that contain more oils or fats and flavours (see Rabbit and Seafood Paella, page 144). The cuts and joints are similar to the other quadrupeds/mammals and can be fried, roasted, rolled or braised in much the same way.

Feather game

These birds are plucked and drawn (gutted) just like poultry. They are best roasted whole, as the individual pieces are small and fiddly, or deboned and cubed for casseroles, such as Pheasant and Gammon Pie (see page 143) or stir-frying.

WEEKNIGHT SUPPERS

CHICKEN KIEVS

When buying chicken breasts for this, find the largest and plumpest possible; it will really help with keeping the garlic butter in the middle. If you're cutting your own whole chicken, remove the breast joints from the bone (see pages 69–71). Free-range chicken breasts are noticeably better for this recipe from a practical as well as ethical point of view. They aren't pumped with water or flushed with too much water in the plucking stage, so they won't shrivel, which would make the garlic butter leak or release water into the oil so that it doesn't brown.

2 large, skinless, free-range chicken breasts

1 teaspoon freshly chopped tarragon

40 g/5 tablespoons plain/all-purpose flour

3 eggs, beaten

100 g/2 cups dried breadcrumbs

300 ml/1¼ cups sunflower oil, for frying

salad leaves and Buttery Crushed Potatoes (see page 217), to serve

GARLIC BUTTER

50 g/3½ tablespoons butter, softened

1 garlic clove, finely chopped

2 big pinches of freshly chopped parsley

a squeeze of lemon juice (approximately ¼ lemon; save the rest to serve)

salt and black pepper, to season

SERVES 2

Start by mixing the garlic butter so you can chill it in the fridge to harden. Mix the butter, garlic, parsley and lemon juice in a bowl, and season with salt and pepper. Portion the butter into two flat, thin pieces, approximately 2 cm/1 inch wide and 4 cm/2 inches long, so that they'll slot into the cut in the chicken breast. Wrap in foil and put in the fridge to harden while you prepare the chicken.

Cut the 'false fillet' (the small piece of muscle on the side, which is attached can be prized apart by pulling it) off the chicken breasts, as you're going to use this to plug the hole in the side.

Lay each breast flat, push down on the top to level it and carefully slice through the middle, front to back, so that there's a cut down one side. Don't cut all the way through; the cut needs to go about three-quarters of the way through.

Take the garlic butter from the fridge and place a piece inside each breast. Take the false fillet and push one end in first, at the edge of the cut, then slot the other end into the other end of the cut to help 'plug' it.

Mix the tarragon with the flour. Roll each stuffed breast in the seasoned flour, dip in the egg and then cover really well with breadcrumbs. You can then fry it straight away, but I like to double-dip! Wrap in foil and place in the fridge for 30 minutes for it to 'set'.

Take the kievs out of the fridge and repeat the coating process: flour first, then egg and then breadcrumbs.

Heat the sunflower oil in a heavy-bottomed pan or deep-fryer until a cube of bread browns in 20 seconds. Carefully lower the kievs into the hot oil and fry for 20 minutes, or until cooked through, turning carefully once halfway through cooking.

Drain on paper towels, then serve with a lemon quarter to squeeze over the top, salad leaves and buttery crushed potatoes, if you like.

CHICKEN TIKKA MASALA

Many polls have concluded that chicken tikka masala is the most popular dish in the UK and it's also a much-loved Indian dish in the USA, so let's see if I can do its popularity justice. It's a great one to batch-cook and portion, too, and it's delicious cold for lunch. If you're cutting your own chicken, dice the breasts and use the boneless thigh meat (see pages 69–71).

4 teaspoons olive oil

1 red onion, diced

1 garlic clove, finely chopped

4 chicken breasts (or 2 breasts and 2 boneless thighs), diced

1 red chilli/chile, deseeded and finely chopped

a pinch of ground ginger

a pinch of ground turmeric

a pinch of ground cumin

a pinch of paprika

freshly squeezed juice of ½ lime (the rest can be cut for serving)

3 tablespoons tomato purée/paste

a big pinch of freshly chopped coriander/cilantro, plus extra whole leaves to garnish

1 teaspoon soft dark brown sugar

200 g/7 oz. canned chopped tomatoes

5 tablespoons double/heavy cream

salt and black pepper, to season

cooked basmati rice and naan bread, to serve

SERVES 4

Heat the oil in a pan set over a high heat and fry the onion and garlic for about 5 minutes until they start to brown.

Add the diced chicken, the chilli/chile, all the pinches of scrummy seasoning, a pinch of salt and pepper, and the lime juice (if you cut the lime lengthways, you can make longer wedges with the other half to serve – it's easier to squeeze).

Stir in the tomato purée/paste, coriander/cilantro and sugar. Lastly, add the chopped tomatoes and double/heavy cream.

Bring to the boil, then reduce the heat to low and simmer for 15–20 minutes, until the chicken is cooked through.

Taste and check the seasoning. A good trick is to taste the sauce and then smell each of the seasonings – your nose will tell you whether you want to add a pinch more of anything or just a little salt and pepper.

Serve with rice and naan bread, and a sprinkling of extra whole coriander/cilantro leaves.

PERFECTLY TENDER PORK CHOPS

Pork loin chops are a delicious and very quick meat dish – they can be fancy for entertaining or just quick and easy for a weeknight supper. One thing that is often a challenge, though, is keeping them soft. Of course, I'm going to say again (every time!) that if you start with well-farmed pork, more than half the work is done for you, which makes it so much easier to impress with your skills... but there's also a good method for cooking this pork that will really ensure it is soft and succulent, and it's always fun to get a few flames going in the kitchen...

2 tablespoons olive oil

1 white onion, sliced

2 sticks/ribs celery, strings peeled and sliced

a big pinch of freshly chopped parsley

2 pork chops

3½ tablespoons brandy

100 ml/7 tablespoons cider

100 ml/7 tablespoons Brown or White Chicken Stock (see page 32) or 1 tablespoon jellied stock

3 tablespoons crème fraîche or sour cream (optional)

grated zest and freshly squeezed juice of 1 lemon (optional)

salt and black pepper, to season

SERVES 2

Heat half of the oil in a frying pan/skillet set over a medium heat and fry the onion and celery with some salt and pepper and the parsley for 5 minutes. Transfer to a plate and set aside.

Put the other half of the oil in the pan and, over a high heat, fry the pork chops for 30 seconds on each side to brown the surfaces.

Pour in the brandy and set alight (tilt the pan to ignite if you're using a gas hob/stovetop, or use a match to light the brandy if you're using an electric hob/stovetop). This is called 'flambéing' – the flames burn off the alcohol to soften the flavour of the brandy as well as leave behind the flavour of flash-heated pork that you wouldn't get from just simmering the chops. It also looks cool.

Let the flames die down and then pour in the cider and the stock, and let boil for 5 minutes.

Reduce the heat to medium, half-cover with a lid or piece of foil and leave gently bubbling for 10 minutes (or 15 minutes if they're thick chops).

Make a slice in one of the chops to check that they're cooked through and not pink at all. Cook for a few minutes more if not.

You can make a simple sauce here by spooning in crème fraîche and adding the lemon zest and juice, or just serve the pork chops as they are.

PORK MEDALLIONS AND LINGUINE

If you're cutting the pork shoulder at home, this recipe is great using the neck fillet as well, or buy a fillet/tenderloin or pre-cut medallions, about 2 cm/¾ inch thick.

40 g/3 tablespoons butter

1 garlic clove

4 rashers/strips of bacon (smoked bacon is great for flavour, if you like the smoky taste), chopped

6 spring onions/scallions, trimmed and chopped

4 asparagus spears (optional)

a big pinch of freshly chopped tarragon

4 pork medallions

100 ml/scant ½ cup white wine

340 g/12 oz. linguine

200 ml/¾ cup crème fraîche or sour cream

salt and black pepper, to season

freshly chopped flat-leaf parsley, to garnish

SERVES 4

Heat the butter in a ridged griddle pan (or a frying pan/skillet is fine if you don't have a griddle pan).

Fry the garlic, bacon, spring onions/scallions and asparagus (if using) for a minute to mix with the butter and coat the pan.

Add a pinch of salt and pepper and the tarragon.

Use a wooden spoon or other utensil to clear four spaces in the pan and add the pork medallions to the spaces in the pan. Cook over a high heat for about 2 minutes on each side.

Turn the heat down to medium and add the white wine. Cover with a lid or piece of kitchen foil and cook for a further 12 minutes, turning the pork pieces again halfway through. Meanwhile, start cooking the linguine in a large pan of salted water following the packet instructions.

Once the pork is cooked, put the four pieces on a plate and set aside for a moment.

Drain the linguine and stir in the crème fraîche. Then tip in the mixture from the griddle pan and stir to coat the pasta in the creamy sauce. Spoon the linguine into four pasta bowls and place a piece of pork on the top.

Add a crunch of black pepper and some chopped parsley to garnish, and serve with a cold beer.

PORK AND APPLE SLIDERS

For anyone who doesn't know, a 'slider' is a mini burger and it makes a great canapé for entertaining or a lovely choice for children's plates. They are usually served in mini bread rolls, but this recipe uses fried potato discs instead – happily use either, depending on what you fancy.

10 g/2 teaspoons butter

50 g/½ cup finely diced dessert or cooking apple

180 g/6 oz. really good pork mince/ground pork (see page 27 for hand-mincing/hand-cutting)

10 g/2 teaspoons dried breadcrumbs

10 g/2 teaspoons tomato purée/paste

a pinch of freshly chopped parsley

salt and black pepper, to season

POTATO 'BUNS'

4 new potatoes

10 g/2 teaspoons butter

MAKES 4

Heat the butter in a frying pan/skillet over a medium heat and fry the diced apple pieces for about 6 minutes until they brown and start to go sticky.

Remove the apple from the pan and set on a plate to cool (you can chill a plate in the fridge before you start to help speed this up). Don't worry about washing up the pan – we're going to use it again.

Mix the pork mince/ground pork with a pinch of salt, the breadcrumbs, tomato purée/paste and parsley really well in a bowl. Add the apple pieces once they've cooled a bit and mix.

Divide the mixture in half and then in half again to get four even pieces (weighing approximately 60 g/2 oz. each). Shape and flatten each portion – flatter sliders are easier to cook and serve.

Meanwhile, for the potatoes, bring a pan of water to the boil. Leave the skins on the new potatoes and slice them, not too thin, approximately 1 cm/½ inch thick. You need two slices per slider, but I would make a few spares in case any break... and to nibble whilst the sliders are cooking later... you'll see what I mean! Perhaps make 12 slices to be on the safe side.

Add the potato slices to the boiling water and parboil them for just 2 minutes to soften. Drain and set aside.

Heat the butter in the same frying pan/skillet from earlier over a medium heat and pick out the best-looking potato slices to fry with a good crack of black pepper.

Fry well and then set aside on a wire rack or paper towel, with the slices not touching each other to keep them crispy.

Add the sliders to the same pan and fry for 3–4 minutes on each side, until cooked through. This is when you want to nibble a potato slice, is that right?

To serve, put a slider between two potato slices and use a cocktail stick/toothpick to keep the slider together, then serve.

TOAD IN THE HOLE

An absolute favourite in my house growing up, and a special treat on a Saturday if our grandma came for lunch... Grandma would then explain that she had 'far too much' and we would get to eat the rest of hers. An even better result all round!

140 g/1 cup plain/all-purpose flour

2 eggs, beaten

150 ml/generous ½ cup milk

150 ml/generous ½ cup water

25 g/2 tablespoons butter

8 good-quality, thick pork sausages (to make your own skinless sausages, see below)

salt and black pepper, to season

Red Onion Gravy (opposite), to serve

HOMEMADE SKINLESS SAUSAGES

500 g/1 lb. 2 oz. good-quality pork mince/ground pork (see page 27 for hand-mincing/hand-cutting)

½ teaspoon salt

25 g/1 tablespoon dried breadcrumbs

20 g/4 teaspoons tomato purée/paste

1 egg, beaten

a pinch of freshly chopped parsley

a 25 x 35-cm/10 x 14-inch roasting pan, greased

SERVES 4 (OR 4½ WITH GRANDMA!)

Whizz the flour, a pinch of salt, the eggs, milk and water together in a food processor to make a batter. Put in the fridge to rest for at least 30 minutes.

Preheat the oven to 180°C (350°F) Gas 4.

Heat the butter in a frying pan/skillet over a medium–high heat and fry the sausages so that they're browned all over – don't worry about the middle not being fully cooked here, as they'll be baked later in the batter; this is just to brown them for flavour.

Place the browned sausages evenly in the base of the greased pan and pour the batter over the top.

Bake in the preheated oven for 45 minutes, but check it after 30 minutes; if the batter is crisping already, turn the temperature down and only bake for a further 5 minutes; if it hasn't started to crisp yet, turn up to 200°C (400°F) Gas 6 for the last 15 minutes.

Season with salt and pepper and serve with red onion gravy.

Homemade Skinless Sausages

Mix the pork mince/ground pork and salt first of all until the mince becomes sticky (this is the salt breaking down the proteins in the pork and will help with texture and binding). Mix in the rest of the ingredients and a pinch of pepper and shape into eight sausage shapes. Use as above, frying them gently so that they don't break up in the pan.

FAGGOTS WITH RED ONION GRAVY

Faggots don't have a great reputation. They need a big marketing campaign or maybe we all just need to try making them and learn how delicious, simple and great value they are. If there is ever a recipe for the modern meat budget, this is it.

1 whole pig pluck (the heart, lungs, liver and kidneys of a pig), trimmed

100 g/3½ oz. streaky/fatty bacon, chopped

200 g/7 oz. pork mince/ground pork (see page 27 for hand-mincing/hand-cutting)

120 g/¾ cup porridge oats/oatmeal

30 g/2 tablespoons tomato purée/paste

1 red onion, finely chopped

2 eggs, beaten

a big pinch each of freshly chopped parsley, sage and thyme

a big pinch each of nutmeg, allspice and cayenne pepper

salt and black pepper, to season

Buttery Crushed Potatoes or Fancy Mashed Potatoes (see page 217), to serve

RED ONION GRAVY

20 g/4 teaspoons butter

4 red onions, finely sliced

1 tablespoon brown sugar

2 tablespoons red wine vinegar

250 ml/1 cup Brown or White Chicken Stock (see page 32)

a pinch each of freshly chopped or dried sage and tarragon

a pinch of salt

baking parchment, greased with butter (optional)

SERVES 4

Preheat the oven to 170°C (325°F) Gas 3.

Trim any hard or dark blood parts off the pluck and cut it into pieces. (I like to use only half of the liver, or one-third if it's a very large pluck, as it's the strongest flavour and can overpower the other elements, but it's totally up to you.)

Bring a large pan of water to the boil and boil the pluck for 20 minutes. Drain well, chop into small pieces and transfer to a mixing bowl.

Add all the other ingredients with a pinch of salt and pepper, and mix with your hands until it's really soft. Shape into a big, long sausage and then cut into eight pieces. Roll the pieces into balls.

Like with homemade haggis (see page 98), I bake these in baking parchment, so that they're soft inside and slightly crisp on the outside, but you can bake them as they are for a crisp outside. Put a faggot on each sheet of greased baking parchment and twist the ends like a sweet/candy wrapper, if you want to bake them in parchment.

Bake in the preheated oven for 50 minutes, until cooked through. Season with salt and pepper and serve with buttery crushed potatoes or fancy mashed potatoes.

Red Onion Gravy

Heat the butter in a pan over a medium heat and fry the onions until they are very soft and browning. Stir in the sugar until it's dissolved and sticky. Add the red wine vinegar, stir well and then slowly pour in the chicken stock. Add the sage, tarragon and a pinch of salt, and keep stirring over the heat until it thickens.

PORK STROGANOFF

Such an easy one-pot dish and a great use of pork shoulder. It's great with all the easiest accompaniments like rice, potatoes or pasta, so it's a perfect one to make in a larger batch and freeze in portions for easy lunches and dinners.

15 g/1 tablespoon butter

1 small white onion, diced

1 garlic clove, chopped

110 g/1½ cups mushrooms, sliced

200 g/7 oz. pork shoulder, diced (see pages 27 and 61–65)

1 teaspoon wholegrain mustard

a pinch of freshly chopped parsley

a pinch of freshly chopped tarragon

4 tablespoons double/heavy cream

1 tablespoon brandy

Fancy Mashed Potatoes (see page 217) and some green vegetables, to serve

salt and black pepper, to taste

SERVES 2

Heat the butter in a pan over a medium heat and fry the onion, garlic and mushrooms until they start to brown. Add a pinch of salt and pepper and then the diced pork. Continue to fry for 4–5 minutes to cook the pork through.

Stir in the mustard, parsley, tarragon, cream and brandy. Reduce the heat to low, pop a lid on top and simmer. For this two-portion quantity, it will need only 15–20 minutes; for a larger batch, double the time and just give it a stir occasionally until the sauce thickens.

Serve hot with potatoes (my favourite with this is mashed) and greens seasoned to taste with salt and pepper. Or, cool the mixture right down and portion in sealed containers or sandwich bags and freeze for up to 3 months.

SWEET CHILLI PORK BELLY AND NOODLES

The crispier the better for these pork pieces. I like to make the pieces really dark and crunchy, and adding the lime towards the end of frying is a great way to crisp them up and perfect the balance with the sweetness.

400 g/14 oz. rindless pork belly, diced

1 red chilli/chile, deseeded and finely chopped, plus extra to serve (optional)

2 tablespoons clear honey

2 teaspoons ground paprika

1 garlic clove, finely chopped

1 tablespoon sesame oil

1 tablespoon vegetable oil

8–10 spring onions/scallions, trimmed and finely sliced

1 red (bell) pepper, deseeded and finely chopped

2 pak choi/bok choy, trimmed and chopped

1 tablespoon plain/all-purpose flour

a pinch each of salt and black pepper

freshly squeezed juice of 1 lime, plus 1 lime, cut into wedges, to serve

noodles and soy sauce, to serve

SERVES 2

A few hours in advance, or the day before, marinate the pork belly to really give it flavour. Put the diced, rindless belly pieces in a bag or bowl with the chilli/chile, honey, paprika, garlic and sesame oil. Seal and leave in the fridge for a few hours or overnight.

Heat the vegetable oil in a wok or high-sided frying pan/skillet and fry the spring onions/scallions, red (bell) pepper and pak choi/bok choy over a high heat until they are soft and starting to brown. Transfer them to a plate and set aside.

Spoon the belly pieces out of the marinade (keep the marinade) and coat them in the flour. Add to the wok and fry over a high heat until they become crisp (and smell amazing!), then add the marinade and fry for 4–5 minutes until the pork is cooked through.

Squeeze in the lime juice to help them crisp some more. Return the cooked vegetables to the wok along with a pinch of salt and pepper. Stir well, then serve with noodles and soy sauce. Sprinkle some more chopped red chilli/chile on the top to add an extra fresh kick, if you like.

ROGAN JOSH

This is such a quick and easy weeknight supper... though I think it has the longest and most tantalizing list of herbs and seasonings in the whole book, showing perfectly that speedy or easy recipes don't have to lack a flavour punch.

400 g/14 oz. diced lamb rump (see pages 53–56 to cut the rump from a leg of lamb)

2 tablespoons olive oil

2 garlic cloves

a 2-cm/1-inch piece of peeled fresh ginger, or 1 teaspoon ground ginger

1 teaspoon ground cinnamon

a pinch of fennel seeds

1 teaspoon ground cumin

1 teaspoon ground coriander

½ teaspoon chilli/chili powder

2 bay leaves

200 ml/scant 1 cup Greek-style yogurt

1 teaspoon garam masala

4 handfuls of spinach leaves (optional)

boiled rice, a pinch of saffron, a pinch of salt and some freshly squeezed lime juice, to serve

a big pinch paprika and a little fresh coriander/cilantro, to garnish

SERVES 2

Trim the lamb well so that it's nice and lean, as we won't be cooking this for very long.

Heat the olive oil in a frying pan/skillet and start by browning the garlic, ginger and diced lamb over a medium heat. Add the cinnamon, fennel seeds, cumin, coriander, chilli/chili powder and bay leaves and mix well.

Stir in the yogurt, then add the garam masala. Reduce the heat to low and simmer for 5 minutes.

Mix in the spinach leaves, if using, and cook until soft.

To serve, season some plain rice with a pinch of saffron, salt and a big squeeze of lime juice. Spoon over the rogan josh, sprinkle a little ground paprika on the top and garnish with a little fresh coriander/cilantro. Accompany with a cold lager or perhaps a chilled, fruity rosé wine.

LAMB AND ROSEMARY MEATBALLS

This is a lovely way to flavour and cook lamb mince. If you're cutting your own lamb leg, follow the instructions on page 27 to hand-mince/hand-cut the trim.

400 g/14 oz. lamb mince/ground lamb (see page 27 for hand-mincing/hand-cutting)

30 g/2 tablespoons dried breadcrumbs

30 g/2 tablespoons tomato purée/paste

a pinch of freshly chopped rosemary, or ½ teaspoon dried rosemary

1 garlic clove, very finely chopped

½ teaspoon mustard powder

20 g/4 teaspoons butter, for frying

a pinch of salt and black pepper

cooked pasta, to serve

SAUCE (OPTIONAL)
5 tablespoons white wine

200 ml/scant 1 cup crème fraîche or sour cream

a big pinch of freshly chopped parsley

MAKES 16 MEATBALLS

Mix the lamb, breadcrumbs, tomato purée/paste, rosemary, garlic, mustard powder, salt and pepper together well in a bowl. Divide the mixture into 16 meatballs – the easiest way to make these even is to shape the mixture into a ball, halve it, halve each of those, then again and again, so you have 16 meatballs. It's easier to halve pieces by sight and feel than to take off a meatball piece at a time.

To cook the meatballs, put the butter in a frying pan/skillet and fry on a medium–high heat for 10–12 minutes until browned and cooked through.

For a simple sauce, add the wine to the frying pan/skillet once the meatballs are cooked. Bring to a boil, then add the remaining sauce ingredients and season with salt and pepper. Serve with pasta.

LAMB, OLIVE AND FETA BURGERS

I love these burgers because they're juicy, but still quite light and fresh-tasting. Perfect for serving on warm summer evenings.

500 g/1 lb. 2 oz. lamb mince/ground lamb (see page 27 for hand-mincing/hand-cutting)

60 g/4 tablespoons dried breadcrumbs

1 egg, beaten

50 g/½ cup pitted black olives, chopped

50 g/2 oz. feta cheese, crumbled

30 g/2 tablespoons tomato purée/paste

a big pinch of freshly chopped parsley

1 garlic clove, finely chopped

2 teaspoons olive oil, plus extra for frying

4 pitta breads, shredded romaine lettuce, sour cream and lemon wedges, to serve

salt and black pepper, to taste

MAKES 4 BURGERS

Mix all the ingredients, apart from those to serve, in a bowl really well, squeezing the mixture together to help it to bind.

Split the mixture in half, and then half each again to make four even burger patties. Flatten them down and try to make the thickness as even as possible.

Heat a little olive oil in a frying pan/skillet over a high heat and lay the burgers in the oil. Fry for 30 seconds each side, then turn the heat down to medium and fry for a further 5 minutes on each side.

These are delicious in pitta breads with shredded romaine lettuce, sour cream and a squeeze of fresh lemon juice. Season with salt and pepper to taste.

SHEPHERD'S PIE

Shepherd's pie uses lamb mince, whereas cottage pie uses beef mince – but in my opinion this comforting pie is lovely with either. The porridge oats help to make the mixture soft and squishy but stop it from going slimy, which flour can sometimes do when you use it to thicken the base of a pie.

600 g/1 lb. 5 oz. all-purpose potatoes, such as Maris Piper or Yukon Gold, peeled and chopped into 2-cm/1-inch chunks

1 garlic clove

2 carrots, chopped

1 white onion, chopped

45 g/3 tablespoons butter

500 g/1 lb. 2 oz. lamb mince/ ground lamb (see page 27 for hand-mincing/hand-cutting)

20 g/4 teaspoons tomato purée/paste

200 ml/scant 1 cup red wine

150 ml/²/₃ cup vegetable stock

a pinch of dried rosemary

a pinch of dried thyme

40 g/generous ⅓ cup old-fashioned rolled oats

50 ml/3½ tablespoons milk

20 g/⅓ cup finely grated Parmesan, plus extra for sprinkling on top (optional)

salt and black pepper, to season

a 20 x 25-cm/8 x 10-inch ovenproof dish, greased

SERVES 4

Preheat the oven to 180°C (350°F) Gas 4.

Bring a large pan of water to the boil and boil the potatoes for about 20 minutes, until soft enough to mash.

Meanwhile, heat 15 g/1 tablespoon of the butter in a frying pan/ skillet over a medium heat and add the garlic, carrots and onion. Fry for about 4–5 minutes, until softened and starting to brown.

Add the lamb and fry until cooked, breaking it up as it cooks using a wooden spoon.

Add the tomato purée/paste and stir in. Then add the red wine, vegetable stock, rosemary, thyme and some salt and pepper. Stir well and then add the oats, a little at a time. Mix well and cook, stirring, until the mixture is nice and thick and the oats have absorbed the liquid.

By now the potatoes should be soft, so drain and mash them, mixing in the milk, Parmesan and remaining 30 g/2 tablespoons of the butter.

Spoon the lamb mixture into the greased ovenproof dish and press down to make it level. Then spread the mashed potatoes over the top evenly.

Put the dish in the preheated oven and bake for 20 minutes. To brown the top, add a little more Parmesan (or sprinkle with grated mature Cheddar) and place under a hot grill/broiler for the last 5 minutes.

HOMEMADE HAGGIS

This is such a delicious, good-value and nutritious meal. I love the full tradition with the offal and stomach casing, but they're not always easy to source, so this has an alternative version to achieve an equally delicious flavour and texture.

75 g/2½ oz. lamb's liver

100 g/3½ oz. each of lamb's heart and lamb's lights/lungs or 200 g/7 oz. lamb mince/ ground lamb (see page 27 for hand-mincing/hand-cutting)

100 g/3½ oz. beef suet or vegetable shortening

a big pinch of allspice

a pinch of cayenne pepper

1 small red onion, finely chopped

1 garlic clove, finely chopped

a big pinch of freshly chopped parsley, plus extra to garnish

1 tablespoon white wine vinegar

30 g/2 tablespoons tomato purée/paste

120 g/¾ cup old-fashioned rolled oats

salt, to season

1 sheep's stomach (alternatively, use baking parchment)

'NEEPS AND TATTIES'

1 swede/rutabaga

2 baking potatoes

a large knob/pat of butter

black pepper, to taste

butcher's string/twine

SERVES 2

Pre-heat the oven to 160°C (325°F) Gas 3.

Finely chop the liver, heart and lights/lungs, if using, or chop the liver and mix it into the lamb mince/ground lamb. Transfer to a mixing bowl and add the chopped suet/vegetable shortening, allspice, salt, cayenne pepper, onion, garlic, parsley, white wine vinegar, tomato purée/paste and oats.

Then either stuff into the stomach and seal the end with butcher's string/twine or squeeze into a tight ball. Place into the centre of a square of baking parchment and twist or tie the ends to lock it in.

Wrap in a layer of foil and place into 1 cm/⅜ inch of water in the bottom of an ovenproof pan. Set a lid on top and cook in the preheated oven for 2 hours. Remove the haggis from the casing, season with salt and slice it to serve.

'Neeps and Tatties'

While your haggis is cooking, you can make your 'neeps and tatties', the accompaniments for this famous Scottish meal. Peel and chop the swede/rutabaga and potatoes into small dice. Boil separately (or together, if you prefer), drain and mash with the butter and freshly ground black pepper.

MUTTON, PEAR AND ROQUEFORT SALAD

I love mutton and this is a lovely way to lighten the richness of the meat in a dressed salad. The sweetness of pear provides the perfect balance.

2 ripe pears, quartered lengthways and cored

40 g/3 tablespoons butter

1 mutton fillet/ tenderloin, about 500 g/1 lb. 2 oz.

4 large handfuls of romaine or Little Gem/ Bibb lettuce leaves

125 g/4½ oz. Roquefort cheese, or other rich and creamy cheese

7-8 fresh basil leaves

salt and black pepper, to taste

DRESSING

2 tablespoons olive oil

1 tablespoon balsamic vinegar

freshly squeezed juice of ½ lime

SERVES 2

Preheat the grill/broiler to high.

Arrange the quartered and cored pears on a baking sheet. Melt half the butter in a frying pan/skillet and drizzle over the pears. Spread it over the top of the pears. Place under the grill/ broiler for 5 minutes.

Meanwhile, heat the rest of the butter in the frying pan/skillet over a high heat. Add the mutton to the pan and roll it in the butter for 5 minutes, until the surface is completely browned. (If you'd prefer your meat more well done, cook it for 10 minutes over a medium heat.) Set aside to rest.

Make the dressing and toss the leaves in it. Divide the leaves between two plates. Tear the cheese into pieces and sprinkle over the top. Layer the grilled/broiled pear on top. Slice the fillet/ tenderloin very thinly using a sharp knife. It should still be pink in the middle. Place on the plates and add a good scrunch of salt and black pepper and a few torn basil leaves.

AFRICAN GOAT AND PLANTAIN CURRY

This African-inspired dish also works well with lamb, mutton or veal.

2 tablespoons olive oil or argan oil

2 garlic cloves, chopped

1 white onion, chopped

a 3-cm/1¼-inch piece of fresh ginger, peeled and grated

1 red chilli/chile, deseeded and chopped

800 g/1 lb. 12 oz. goat loin or shoulder, diced (or use lamb, mutton or veal)

4 green plantains

a big pinch of freshly chopped coriander/ cilantro

6-8 fresh basil leaves

a handful of freshly chopped parsley

2 beef/beefsteak tomatoes, diced

200 ml/scant 1 cup Brown or White Chicken Stock (see page 32)

salt and black pepper, to season

lemon wedges, to serve

a 20-cm/8-inch ovenproof dish, greased

SERVES 4

Preheat the oven to 170°C (350°F) Gas 4.

Heat the oil in a frying pan/skillet over a medium heat and fry the garlic, onion, grated ginger, chilli/chile and a pinch of salt and pepper for a few minutes until soft.

Add the meat and stir to brown all over.

Peel the plantain, halve them lengthways and lay them flat in the base of the prepared ovenproof dish. Put the goat meat and all the mixture from the frying pan/skillet over the top, then cover with the coriander/cilantro, basil, parsley and diced tomatoes. Add the stock. Cover with a lid and cook in the preheated oven for 1 hour.

Remove the lid, stir the mixture away from the sides and just lift the plantain pieces gently off the bottom to make sure they're not catching. Return to the oven, uncovered, for another 30 minutes. Season and serve with wedges of lemon and a cold ginger beer.

CORNISH PASTIES

The smell of these delicious Cornish pasties coming out of the oven is irresistible. The traditional filling of diced beef, swede, carrot and onion is encased in crisp homemade pastry. They are ideal to freeze, as they bake brilliantly from frozen, making them a perfect midweek supper.

500 g/1 lb. 2 oz. diced beef (rump/round is lovely for these, see page 39)

160 g/5½ oz. swede/rutabaga, finely diced

160 g/5½ oz. carrot, finely diced

75 g/2½ oz. onion, finely diced

a pinch of fresh thyme leaves

a pinch each of salt and black pepper

FOR THE PASTRY

500 g/1 lb. 2 oz. butter

1 kg/2 lb. 4 oz. plain/all-purpose flour, plus extra for dusting

cold water, to bind

a pinch each of salt and black pepper

1 beaten egg, to glaze

a 25-cm/10-inch pastry/cookie cutter

MAKES 6 LARGE PASTIES

Preheat the oven to 180°C (350°F) Gas 4.

Make the pastry first by crumbling the butter and flour, plus some salt and pepper together with your fingertips. Then add a little cold water, just a splash at a time, until the pastry comes together.

Sprinkle a little more flour over a work surface and use a rolling pin to roll out the pastry to a thickness of about 5 mm/¼ inch. Use the cutter to cut out six 25-cm/10-inch circles.

Either leave the circles out if you've space or layer them with a little baking parchment in between to keep them separate.

Put the steak, swede/rutabaga, carrot, onion, thyme and some salt and pepper in a bowl and mix well. Divide the filling among the pastry circles and spread it out evenly on the right side of each circle, so that you can fold over the other side. Pull the left side over and press it together to seal 1 cm/½ inch away from the edge of the right hand side of the pastry. This allows a little room to fold the edge back over the fold to seal in the filling nice and tightly.

Lay some baking parchment onto a baking sheet (you can grease this a little with some butter, too, to be safe), slide a palette knife/metal spatula under the pasties and lift them carefully onto the paper.

Bake in the preheated oven for 45 minutes and serve straight away or chill in the fridge for up to a week.

Pastry Tip
You can also wrap the uncooked pastries and filling in clingfilm/plastic wrap or foil and freeze them for up to 3 months, as long as the meat hasn't been previously frozen. It's a really handy thing to have ready in the freezer and bakes perfectly well from frozen in a preheated oven at 160°C (325°F) Gas 3 for 90 minutes.

OVEN MEATLOAF

In the UK, we're way behind the Americans in appreciating the ease, taste and versatility of the unassuming meatloaf. I don't know why it isn't more popular; it will be one day. This is a classic recipe combination but, as with burgers, you can have some fun putting more ingredients in and trying out the hard-boiled/hard-cooked egg in the middle thing. Serve it with your choice of vegetables or chips/fries, or put it in a brioche sandwich with Chunky Barbecue Sauce (see page 111).

150 g/5½ oz. really good beef mince/ground beef (see page 27 for hand-mincing/hand-cutting)

120 g/4 oz. really good pork mince/ground pork (see page 27 for hand-mincing/hand-cutting your own)

50 g/3 tablespoons dried breadcrumbs

50 g/2 oz. white onion, diced

1 teaspoon wholegrain mustard

20 g/4 teaspoons tomato purée/paste

½ garlic clove, chopped

a pinch of dried parsley

½ beaten egg

salt and black pepper, to season

SERVES 2

Preheat the oven to 180°C (350°F) Gas 4.

Mix all the ingredients really well together in a mixing bowl. Shape the whole mixture into a large sausage shape, trying to keep the thickness as even as possible.

There are two tricks for cooking it. Either put a stainless-steel skewer through the middle (lengthways) to help the roasting balance, place it in a roasting pan and roast for 35 minutes. Or wrap it in some baking parchment and twist the ends (like for Homemade Haggis on page 98) and bake it in the oven for 40 minutes.

Leave to stand for 5 minutes so that the juices settle and it is easier to slice. Season with salt and pepper and serve.

THE PERFECT KITCHEN STEAK

How to get the steakhouse taste experience in your own home, whatever your favourite cut.

15 g/1 tablespoon butter

225–340 g/8–12 oz. steak of your choice

salt

a sheet of muslin/cheesecloth (optional)

Colour

The colour of your steak will depend on the packaging. A bright red shade only means that it's been gas-flushed with oxygen to help eliminate as much bacteria as possible in the packaging process and to keep the bright red look. It doesn't do any harm to the meat – it's just a process – but don't be afraid to choose a darker grey-red colour, either unpacked or vacuum-sealed.

Marbling

This is the term given to the intramuscular fat in the meat. It's not a sure sign of quality farming though. Indeed, pumping as much grain and corn into cattle, enough to reach the point just before they get ill and can't digest it, produces the most marbling, so be aware if the marbling is a yellow colour, as this likely suggests the presence of corn and grain. We're looking for bright, white marbling, so it's clean and will dissolve beautifully when you cook it. The marbling is best found in rib-eye and sirloin steaks. You will find some in the fillet/tenderloin, though this cut is celebrated for its lean tenderness with or without marbling.

Labelling

The label should tell you about the breed, feed and hanging. Certain breeds are naturally more inclined to marble, like Aberdeen Angus, so that will help you know whether the marbling has occurred naturally. The feed should proudly say that the animals have been reared mostly on grass and pasture, the things they can digest, with any grain only in the last 10–12 weeks for the optimum yield of marbling. The meat needs to be marbled for the hanging to really have an effect, as the weight and stretch in the meat helps to tenderize these veins of fat, which means they'll dissolve more easily when being cooked, coating the meat in flavour.

Packaging

If you've started with a vacuum-sealed steak, your steak will be wet. This is what kept your steak fresh and why I support this method for the time between abattoir and your fridge, but you need to dry it out before cooking. Drying it out will get rid of the metallic, 'iron' taste in the steak, which is from the coating of blood that remains on the outside of the steak and which cooks first and sticks to the meat. The simplest thing to do is remove it from the packaging about 30 minutes before, pat it with paper towels and leave it on a plate at room temperature (turn it over halfway through if you remember) before cooking it. If you have some muslin/cheesecloth, then it's lovely to wrap it up for up to two days before cooking (and if you want to be really fancy, you could hang it from a shelf in your fridge – see page 134 – so it isn't touching anything). Using quality beef would mean wrapping it isn't vital – it does add to the taste, but just a fraction, so it's mostly just to look fancy. Whatever you do, removing the wet blood from the steak means the first thing you're cooking, and therefore tasting, is meat, not blood.

Cooking

My absolute favourite way to cook a steak is frying or griddling. It celebrates the best of the flavours and is so quick and easy. Get the frying pan/skillet or griddle pan really hot first over a high heat, then put in a scoop of butter and a sprinkle of sea salt and let that just start to brown slightly. The temperature of the butter and pan here is important, so here are a few pointers:

- You're looking for the butter to bubble and just start to brown; too soon and your steak will be greasy.
- If the pan starts to smoke, that's too hot and the steak will scorch and taste burnt, even if the middle is still pink. Just hold the pan off the heat for a minute to let it cool and then return to the heat for 10 seconds and add the steak.

- Don't turn too quickly the first time, do wait for 30 seconds so that the first side tightens and browns and seals in the flavour.
- Don't put a lid on the pan – we don't want any moisture at this stage.
- If you have a nice square griddle pan, then you can do two or three steaks at a time. If you have a round pan, be careful not to do too many steaks at the same time, as they won't cook evenly; you want them evenly placed above the best heat to control the temperature. If you need to fry one at a time, still serve them as they are ready, after resting for 2 minutes, rather than try and keep them warm in the oven – just explain to your guests that staggered presentation means better steaks.

Timings

First cook the steak for 30 seconds on each side on this very high heat, then reduce the heat right down to low–medium and let the steak cook for:

- 30 seconds either side for rare;
- 2 minutes either side for medium;
- 4 minutes either side for well done.

These are for an average 1.5–2-cm/$\frac{1}{2}$–$\frac{3}{4}$-inch thick steaks.

If you're cooking a steak with a spine of fat, such as sirloin or the top cuts of rump/round, then I would recommend using tongs to pick up the steak and hold it on its side for 30 seconds, to crisp up the fat and release even more flavour into the pan for the cooking. Once cooked, remove from the pan and allow to rest for 2 minutes, then sprinkle with a little cracked black pepper.

DIANE SAUCE

A bit of a retro choice for a sauce, as it was a victim of its popularity and was a little overused on menus in the 1950s and '60s. Popular it was, though, and a good freshly made one will remind you why.

1 tablespoon olive oil
1 red onion, finely chopped
1 garlic clove, finely chopped
2 tablespoons Worcestershire sauce
2 tablespoons tomato ketchup
150 ml/⅔ cup double/heavy cream

MAKES ABOUT 150 ML/⅔ CUP
(2–3 SERVINGS)

In the same pan in which you have cooked your steak, put the heat back up to high and add the olive oil.

Fry the onion and garlic for 4–5 minutes until they are brown, then add the Worcestershire sauce and ketchup, and stir well for a minute.

Finally mix in the double/heavy cream and bring back to the boil. Serve with the rested steak.

BÉARNAISE SAUCE

This is a lovely light balance for a steak accompaniment. It takes just a little extra time for the cooling and adding the egg, but it's worth it for a really impressive fresh sauce.

85 g/6 tablespoons butter
2 shallots, chopped
4 tablespoons white wine vinegar
a pinch of soft brown sugar
a pinch of dried tarragon
1 egg yolk
75 g/5⅓ cups butter, melted
a pinch of freshly chopped parsley
salt and black pepper

MAKES ABOUT 150 ML/⅔ CUP
(2–3 SERVINGS)

In the same pan in which you have cooked your steak, put the heat up to medium, melt 10 g/ 2 teaspoons of the butter and fry the shallots for 4–5 minutes until brown.

Add the white wine vinegar, sugar, tarragon and some pepper, and bring to the boil. Cook for 5 minutes to reduce slightly, then remove from the heat and allow to cool.

Strain the sauce through a fine mesh sieve/ strainer into a food processor.

Add the egg yolk and whizz until it changes colour and starts to go fluffy.

Meanwhile, melt the remaining butter over a medium heat. Turn the speed right down and slowly drizzle in the melted butter.

Season with salt and freshly chopped parsley. Serve with the rested steak.

PINK PEPPERCORN SAUCE

Peppercorn sauce is definitely my favourite steak accompaniment, but this one uses pink peppercorns, which have a lovely flavour and are very pretty.

2 teaspoons pink peppercorns
20 g/1½ tablespoons butter
2–3 shallots, finely chopped
a handful of mushrooms, finely chopped
1 tablespoon red wine vinegar
1 tablespoon brandy
100 ml/⅓ cup Beef broth or Brown Chicken Stock (see pages 32–33)
50 ml/3 tablespoons double/heavy cream

MAKES ABOUT 200 ML/GENEROUS ¾ CUP (4 SERVINGS)

First crush the peppercorns with a pestle and mortar (or just in a mixing bowl with the bottom of a shatterproof tumbler or the end of a large rolling pin).

Heat the butter in a frying pan/skillet and fry the shallots until they're soft and brown.

Add the mushrooms and stir until they soften fully, then add the crushed peppercorns and stir.

Pour in the red wine vinegar, brandy and stock, and cook over a high heat for 3–4 minutes, until the sauce has reduced.

Mix in the double/heavy cream and serve with the rested steak.

CHUNKY BARBECUE SAUCE

A poor-quality barbecue sauce can ruin a great plate of meat for me. It's so easy to make it at home and I hope you taste the difference when enjoying fresh barbecue sauce as quickly as I did.

50 g/3½ tablespoons butter
1 onion, chopped
2 teaspoons tomato purée/paste
2 tablespoons soft/packed brown sugar
1 teaspoon paprika
a pinch of chipotle powder
2 teaspoons Worcestershire sauce
1 teaspoon English/hot mustard powder
2 tablespoons white wine vinegar
a pinch each of salt and black pepper

MAKES ABOUT 125 ML/½ CUP (2 SERVINGS)

Melt the butter in a frying pan/skillet over a medium heat, then add the onion and fry until soft and browned. Add the tomato purée/paste, sugar, paprika and chipotle powder, and stir well. Add the Worcestershire sauce, mustard powder and vinegar, and season with salt and pepper, then as soon as it bubbles, pour in 150 ml/⅔ cup water. Increase the heat to high and bring to the boil, then let it boil hard, uncovered, for about 10 minutes, until the mixture reduces and thickens.

Remove from the heat and let cool, then whizz it in a food processor. I like to keep barbecue sauce nice and chunky, but you can keep whizzing until it's smooth, if you prefer.

CHILLI CON CARNE

A great recipe to make in a large batch and freeze in portions. After a quick bit of prep, you can leave this bubbling on the hob for as long as you like. It's a good one for the budget, too, with minced/ground beef, kidney beans and chopped tomatoes, all very inexpensive ingredients to buy.

2 tablespoons olive oil

1 red onion, finely chopped

1 garlic clove, finely chopped

800 g/1 lb. 12 oz. beef mince/ ground beef (see page 27 for hand-mincing/hand-cutting)

1 fresh chilli/chile, deseeded and finely chopped

a pinch of cayenne pepper, plus extra to serve

a pinch of ground cumin

a pinch of ground coriander

2 teaspoons dark muscovado/ molasses sugar

1 tablespoon plain/all purpose flour

a pinch each of salt and black pepper

½ beef stock/bouillon cube (or 30 g/1 oz. veal stock)

a 400-g/14-oz. can kidney beans, drained (drained weight 250 g/9 oz.)

1 tablespoon tomato purée/ paste

100 ml/⅓ cup red wine

200 g/7 oz. canned chopped tomatoes

rice and sour cream, to serve

SERVES 4

Heat the oil in a saucepan or deep frying pan/skillet over a medium heat and fry the onion and garlic for about 4–5 minutes until they start to brown.

Add the beef mince/ground beef and fry for another minute, using a wooden spoon to break up the meat.

Add the chilli/chile, cayenne pepper, cumin, coriander, sugar, flour and some salt and pepper, and stir until it forms a paste. Then slowly crumble in the beef stock/bouillon cube or add the veal stock.

Then add the kidney beans, tomato purée/paste, red wine and chopped tomatoes and bring to the boil.

Once it bubbles, reduce the heat to low and let it simmer for 45 minutes, or up to an hour if you can, so that it thickens.

Serve straight away with rice, a dollop of sour cream and a pinch of cayenne pepper on the top.

Chilli con carne freezes brilliantly: portion it into freezerproof containers or sandwich bags and freeze for up to 3 months. Once defrosted, just check the flavours and add a little chilli/chili powder, salt or cayenne pepper to liven it up a bit if necessary.

CLASSIC BOLOGNESE

I love Bolognese and I love Italian food. Although serving this classic meat ragù with spaghetti is not traditional in Italy, it's a must for me! I think the classic Bolognese has also done more for beef mince/ground beef than any other recipe.

10 g/2 teaspoons butter

½ white onion, finely chopped

1 garlic clove, finely chopped

25 g/scant ½ cup chopped mushrooms

2 rashers/strips streaky/fatty bacon, sliced

300 g/10½ oz. beef mince/ ground beef (I recommend 20% fat, see page 27 for hand-mincing/hand-cutting)

20 g/4 teaspoons tomato purée/paste

200 g/7 oz. canned chopped tomatoes

50 ml/3½ tablespoons red wine

3–4 leaves fresh basil, torn

a pinch of oregano

1 bay leaf

salt and black pepper, to taste

SERVES 2

Heat the butter in a pan over a high heat and start by browning the onion and garlic for 4–5 minutes. Then add the mushrooms and bacon and cook for 4–5 minutes, until brown.

Add the mince (a lot of people start with this, but it's better not to overcook it, as it can go chewy). As soon as it is cooked (it will turn from pink to grey), stir in the tomato purée/paste and cook for a couple of minutes, then stir in the chopped tomatoes, red wine, basil, oregano, bay leaf and some salt and pepper. Mix well, bring to the boil and then reduce the heat right down to low to simmer. Cook for at least 20 minutes, and up to 45 minutes if you can.

If you've time, I'm a big fan of letting bolognese cool and then reheating it to serve – it helps to bring out the richness in the tomatoes and the flavour of the beef. It's not vital, but if you can, make this the day before, then just reheat it on the stovetop for 10 minutes. You can cool it quickly by lowering the pan into a shallow sink of cold water and stirring well. Reheating is not vital, but the strength of the flavours really comes through even more.

It's a great pot to take to heat for lunch as well, as long as I haven't eaten it cold for breakfast, another favourite meaty meal of mine!

SQUIDGY MEATBALLS

So called because they have a mozzarella pearl centre so they go super squidgy when you cook them! This is one of the first recipes I made for our farmers' markets when we started our meat company and it's always been one of our favourite meals to cook at home.

800 g/1 lb. 12 oz. beef mince/ ground beef (see page 27 for hand-mincing/hand-cutting)

200 g/2½ cups dried breadcrumbs

80 g/1 cup freshly grated Parmesan cheese, plus extra to serve

3 tablespoons tomato purée/ paste

1 teaspoon dried oregano

1 teaspoon dried basil

20 mozzarella pearls

a pinch each of salt and black pepper

cooked spaghetti, to serve

TOMATO SAUCE

30 g/2 tablespoons butter

1 garlic clove, chopped

1 white onion, chopped

1 teaspoon ground cinnamon

1 tablespoon tomato purée/ paste

800 g/1¾ lbs. canned chopped tomatoes

a pinch of freshly chopped basil

a pinch each of salt and black pepper

SERVES 4

Make the sauce first so it can cook while you're making the meatballs. Melt half the butter in a pan over a high heat and fry the onion and garlic for 4–5 minutes, until brown. Add the cinnamon and stir well. Add the tomato purée/paste and stir for a couple of minutes, then pour in the chopped tomatoes and stir well. Add some salt and pepper, and the basil, reduce the heat to a simmer and cook for 20 minutes to thicken.

Meanwhile, while the sauce is simmering, make the meatballs. Mix the beef mince/ground beef, breadcrumbs, Parmesan, tomato purée/paste, oregano, basil and some salt and pepper in a bowl with your hands, making sure they combine really well.

Divide the mixture into 20 even portions (about 55 g/2 oz. each), then round each one in your hand and flatten on the work surface. Place a mozzarella pearl in the middle of each one and fold the meat around to seal it in.

Preheat the oven to 180°C (360°F) Gas 4.

By now, the sauce should be cooked well. Remove it from the heat and either keep it chunky or use an electric hand mixer to whizz it up and make it really smooth.

Transfer the sauce to an ovenproof dish and set aside. Return the pan to the stovetop (there's no need to clean it) and set it over a high heat. Put the other half of the butter in (don't worry about any of the sauce that remains stuck to the sides of the pan, as it will all mix together!). Fry the meatballs for 8 minutes, being careful to stir them gently so that the mozzarella stays safely in the middle, until the outsides are browning. Transfer the meatballs to the sauce and bake in the preheated oven for 15 minutes.

Serve with spaghetti and top with a sprinkle of Parmesan and a pinch of black pepper. This dish is lovely with a glass of Chianti for a celebration of Italian delights.

SUPERFOOD BURGERS

These are the ultimate superfood beef burgers, with a tasty hit of protein, iron and antioxidants, as well as vitamins A, B6 and C.

300 g/10½ oz. beef mince/ground beef (see page 27 for hand-mincing/hand-cutting)

1 cooked beetroot/beet, grated

½ cooking apple, peeled and diced

20 g/4 teaspoons tomato purée/paste

1 teaspoon powdered spirulina (optional)

20 g/4 teaspoons dried breadcrumbs (optional)

1 garlic clove, finely chopped

a pinch each of salt and black pepper

oil, for frying

wholemeal/whole-wheat rolls, spinach leaves and some hoummus, to serve

MAKES 2

Mix the beef mince/ground beef, grated beetroot/beet, diced cooking apple, tomato purée/paste, spirulina and breadcrumbs (if using), garlic, salt and pepper together with your hands until well mixed.

Divide the mixture in half and shape into two burgers, making sure they're not too fat, so that it's easier to cook them through.

Heat a little oil in a frying pan/skillet over a high heat and put the burgers in. Don't turn them too quickly; let them sear fully on the first side for 4–5 minutes before you move them. Turn and cook on the other side for 5–6 minutes, until they're cooked thoroughly in the middle.

For extra goodness, serve in a lightly toasted wholemeal/whole-wheat roll with a few spinach leaves and a dollop of hoummus on the top.

MICHAELMAS PIE

The filling for this pie is such a simple throw-together recipe, but it tastes terrific with the sweetness of the redcurrant jelly. It's up to you if you'd like to serve mini pies or make one large pie, but I like mini pies the best!

250 g/9 oz. game, such as venison, rabbit and pheasant, diced (alternatively, diced beef is delicious in this pie too)

25 g/2 tablespoons butter

½ garlic clove, chopped

100 g/1½ cups chopped mushrooms

40 g/generous ¼ cup plain/all-purpose flour

20 g/4 teaspoons tomato purée/paste

100 ml/scant ½ cup red wine

80 ml/⅓ cup Beef Broth (see page 33)

40 g/2 tablespoons redcurrant jelly

a sprig of fresh thyme

2 bay leaves

salt and black pepper, to season

1 beaten egg or 20 ml/4 teaspoons milk, for glazing

greens or salad, to serve (optional)

PASTRY

100 g/7 tablespoons salted butter

225 g/1¾ cups plain/all-purpose flour

a pinch of salt

3–4 tablespoons chilled water

8 individual round pie dishes or a 25 x 20-cm/10 x 8-inch pie dish, greased

MAKES 8 MINI PIES OR 1 LARGE PIE TO SERVE 4

Start by making the pastry. Rub the butter, flour and a little salt together with your fingertips until the mixture resembles breadcrumbs. Then keep adding a little chilled water, a tablespoonful at a time, until you can combine the crumbled mixture into a ball of pastry. Don't add too much water. Wrap in clingfilm/plastic wrap and place in the fridge while you make the pie filling.

Preheat the oven to 180°C (350°F) Gas 4.

Put the diced game, butter, garlic, mushrooms, flour, tomato purée/paste, red wine, stock, redcurrant jelly, thyme, bay leaves and some seasoning into a stewing pot (or a pan with a lid) stir, cover with the lid and cook in the preheated oven for 90 minutes. Every 20 minutes or so, take it out and give it a stir; everything will cook really easily and the mixture will start to thicken. Just make sure the flour hasn't stuck to the side or formed an unintentional dumpling – if it has, break it up with a spoon.

On a flour-dusted work surface roll the pastry out to a thickness of 5 mm/¼ inch using a floured rolling pin. Cut out 8 circles or 1 large circle large enough to cover the base and sides of your pie dish(es) and place them into your pie dish(es). Make sure there's enough pastry left over to make the lid(s).

Remove the filling from the oven, but leave the oven on. Remove the sprig of thyme and bay leaves from the mixture and divide the filling between the pastry-lined pie dish(es).

Use the rest of the pastry to make the lid(s) and place these on top of the pie(s), using a little beaten egg or milk to stick the edges to the lid(s), crimping the pastry together with your fingers.

Brush the remaining beaten egg or milk over the top and use a sharp knife or skewer to make one or two little holes in the middle of the lid(s).

Cook the mini pies in the oven for 25 minutes (or 45 minutes for a large pie), until the pastry is cooked and browning.

It's a lovely rich recipe with the meat and red wine, so serve with some greens or salad, or serve the mini pies on their own as luxurious canapés.

ENTERTAINING

PEPPERED VENISON AND PRUNE TERRINE

This terrine is rich and filling. Follow with a light main if serving as an appetizer or serve as a meal in itself with seasonal roast vegetables or a lightly dressed salad as accompaniments. It's perfect for portioning into lunches, too.

a 600-g/1¼-lb. piece of boneless venison (steak or loin)

2 teaspoons olive oil, plus extra for greasing

1–2 bay leaves

2 tablespoons butter, at room temperature

1 garlic clove, crushed

1 egg, beaten

3½ tablespoons double/heavy cream

1 teaspoon wholegrain mustard

1 tablespoon brandy

10 dried, stoned/pitted prunes, roughly chopped

1 teaspoon fresh thyme leaves

1 teaspoon freshly chopped tarragon

6–8 rashers/strips smoked streaky/fatty bacon

salt and black pepper, to season

toasted and buttered ciabatta and dressed mixed salad leaves, to serve

a 20 x 10-cm/8 x 4-in. loaf pan, greased with butter

SERVES 4

Preheat the oven to 180°C (350°F) Gas 4.

Cut 200 g/7 oz. of venison off the piece, ideally widthways so it's as thin a piece as possible, cover and reserve until needed.

Secure a large piece of foil in a roasting pan or on a baking sheet. Set the larger piece of venison on the foil and rub in the olive oil using your hands. Add a few generous pinches of freshly ground black pepper, place the bay leaf/leaves on top, wrap the foil over the top to form a parcel and seal.

Transfer to the preheated oven and roast for 30 minutes.

Remove the venison from the oven, unwrap it, discard the bay leaf/leaves and shred the cooked meat. The easiest way to do this is with two forks. Keep as much of the peppered oil in the shredded meat as you can. Cover and set aside to cool.

When you are ready to bake the terrine, preheat the oven to 180°C (350°F) Gas 4.

Trim any fat off the reserved piece of raw venison and dice the flesh into very small pieces.

Combine the butter, garlic, egg, cream, mustard, brandy, prunes, thyme, tarragon and a pinch of salt in a mixing bowl and lightly beat with a wooden spoon to combine. Add the shredded, peppered venison to the bowl and mix until well combined before adding and mixing in the diced raw venison.

Lay the bacon across the width of the prepared loaf pan, leaving the ends overhanging. Leave a small gap between them so that the terrine is easier to slice when cooked. Spoon the venison mixture into the pan and press down firmly with the back of a spoon. Fold over the overhanging bacon to seal. Cover with a sheet of oiled foil, press down firmly and bake in the middle of the preheated oven for 50 minutes.

Remove the terrine from the oven and cool it as quickly as possible, either by an open window if it's cold outside or partially submerge it in a sink of cold water, making sure the water doesn't seep inside the pan, for the first 30 minutes and then transfer to the fridge. Don't serve the terrine until it has cooled completely and set.

Remove the terrine from the fridge 20 minutes before serving to bring the temperature up a little and bring out the flavours. Slice and serve with toasted ciabatta and a simply dressed salad.

PÂTÉ DE CAMPAGNE

This French classic is easy to make and ideal served as a cold appetizer or a simple yet sophisticated lunch. The recipe makes terrific use of the diced cuts of a pork shoulder if you're cutting your own (see pages 27 and 61–65). It takes a good few hours to set, so is best made the day before you intend to serve it.

2 tablespoons butter

2 tablespoons brandy

4 shallots, finely chopped

1 garlic clove, finely chopped

1 egg, beaten

4 tablespoons double/heavy cream

½ teaspoon Dijon mustard

1 teaspoon finely chopped fresh parsley

1 teaspoon finely chopped fresh tarragon

400 g/14 oz. pork loin (as lean as possible)

6 slices prosciutto

2 hard-boiled/hard-cooked eggs, peeled (optional)

salt and black pepper, to season

oatcakes, crispbread or fried green beans, to serve

a 20 x 10-cm/8 x 4-inch loaf pan, greased with butter

an ovenproof roasting pan, large enough to hold the loaf pan

SERVES 4

Preheat the oven to 180°C (350°F) Gas 4.

Melt the butter in a frying pan/skillet over a medium heat, then add the brandy. Let it come to the boil and then reduce for 1 minute.

Add the shallots and garlic to the pan. Once those have softened, remove the pan from the heat and let cool.

Combine the egg, cream, mustard, parsley and tarragon in a mixing bowl and season with salt and pepper.

Trim any remaining fat from the pork and dice it. (Note: as this recipe isn't cooked for very long in the oven, there isn't time for the fat to break down, so the leaner the meat the better.)

Add the cooled shallot mixture and juices from the pan to the other ingredients in the mixing bowl and stir to combine.

Lay the prosciutto across the width of the prepared loaf pan, leaving the ends overhanging. Leave a small gap between them so that the pâté is easier to slice when cooked. Spoon half of the pork mixture into the prepared pan and, if using the eggs, lay these on top of the mixture now.

Spoon the remainder of the pork mixture on top and fold over the overhanging prosciutto to seal. Cover tightly with oiled kitchen foil.

Put the loaf pan inside the roasting pan and carefully pour about 2.5 cm/1 inch cold water around it. Transfer to the preheated oven and cook for 1 hour, until the meat is firm to the touch. Don't worry if there is liquid around the edge of the pâté or melted butter on the top, as this will set as it cools.

Leave the pâté to cool to the touch before moving to the fridge to cool completely and set – this will take a few hours so, if possible, leave it overnight.

Remove the pâté from the fridge 20 minutes before serving to bring the temperature up a little and bring out the flavours. Slice and serve with oatcakes or crispbread, or try a slice of it on a bed of fried green beans for a warm dish.

CHICKEN LIVER PÂTÉ

I'm in the habit of grabbing lunch on the go. I eventually realized that a chunk of cheese and some bread wasn't keeping me going through the afternoon and it wasn't particularly interesting or memorable to eat. I now find a pâté of any sort is a good option for me, as it's nutritious as well as being utterly delicious. I usually enjoy this recipe spread on some freshly made wholemeal/whole-wheat toast.

45 g/3 tablespoons butter

2 shallots, finely chopped

1 garlic clove, chopped

75 g/3 oz. rindless pork belly, diced

200 g/7 oz. chicken livers, chopped

1 teaspoon freshly chopped thyme, plus a few leaves to garnish

1 tablespoon brandy

1 bay leaf

freshly squeezed lemon juice, to taste

black and pink peppercorns, to garnish (optional)

salt and black pepper, to season

wholemeal/whole-wheat toast, to serve

4 x 150-ml/5-oz. capacity ramekins or similar small ovenproof dishes

SERVES 4

Melt half the butter in a frying pan/skillet set over a medium heat. Add the shallots and garlic and fry for 1 minute.

Add the pork belly, chicken livers, thyme, brandy and a pinch each of salt and pepper, and stir well.

Add the bay leaf to the mixture. Cook for 10 minutes, stirring, until everything is browned and the chicken livers and pork are cooked through.

Remove the pan from the heat and leave to cool until the mixture is warm but not hot.

Remove and discard the bay leaf and then transfer the mixture to a food processor (don't wash the pan just yet, you'll use it again). Add a squeeze of lemon juice to the mixture and whizz until blended. It's up to you how smooth you want it. I like it quite smooth, but you can keep it coarse by stopping just as the mixture starts to stick to the sides of the processor.

Spoon the mixture into the ramekins, leaving about 5 mm/¼ inch at the top.

Melt the rest of the butter in the original frying pan/skillet set over a medium heat, until it starts to bubble. Remove from the heat and carefully pour over the top of each ramekin of pâté. Decorate with a sprinkling of thyme leaves and some black and pink peppercorns, if using.

Transfer the ramekins to the fridge and allow at least 1 hour for the butter to set before serving with wholemeal/whole-wheat toast. The pâté will keep for up to 9 days in the fridge if the seal is unbroken. Eat within 3 days if you break the butter.

You can also freeze the pâté in the ramekins for up to 3 months (before sealing with butter) by wrapping each one in clingfilm/plastic wrap. If you do this, it's best to defrost them in the fridge slowly overnight before serving rather than with any heat or microwaving. You can still pour melted butter on top after defrosting, or just enjoy them without.

GAME RILLETTES

A traditional way of preserving meat in fat, rillettes are a delicious alternative to a heartier terrine and one of my favourite ways to enjoy game. It really celebrates the flavours as well as extending the shelf-life and tenderizing the meat. I've tried this recipe with pheasant, duck, pigeon and rabbit and it works really well for each.

200 g/7 oz. boneless game meat of your choice (see recipe introduction), diced

100 g/3½ oz. pork belly (this is optional but especially recommended for pigeon and rabbit, as they're more lean)

1 tablespoon salt (preferably sea salt flakes or crystals)

25 g/2 tablespoons butter

1 garlic clove, finely chopped

1 bay leaf

a sprig of fresh rosemary

1 teaspoon finely chopped fresh parsley

100 ml/⅓ cup white wine

100 ml/⅓ cup White or Brown Chicken Stock (see page 32), or made from a stock cube

freshly squeezed juice of 1 lemon (if using duck or pigeon, use juice of ½ lemon plus 1 orange instead), plus extra to season

black pepper, to season

crusty baguette and butter, to serve

2 x 150-ml/5-oz. capacity ramekins or similar small ovenproof dishes

SERVES 2

Put the diced game and pork belly in a mixing bowl and add the salt. Massage the salt into the meats really well then cover and leave for a minimum of 2 hours to allow the salt to break down the proteins and start to soften the meat.

Drain away the resulting liquid, rinse the meat and dry with paper towels.

Heat the butter in a frying pan/skillet over a medium heat and brown the meat for 5 minutes.

Add the garlic, herbs, white wine and stock to the pan. Bring to the boil and then reduce the heat to a gentle simmer, cover the pan with a lid and leave for 1½ hours. (Note: for rabbit and pigeon, check the pan after 1 hour. If you can shred the meat at this stage, remove it from the heat – you don't want it to be dry.)

Remove the pan from the heat, add the lemon juice (and orange juice, if using) and stir. Discard the bay leaf and rosemary sprig and leave to cool.

Once it's cold enough to handle, use your fingers to tear up the meats. You can use two forks for this but I find fingers are best.

Taste and adjust the seasoning to taste with black pepper and lemon juice. Spoon the meat into the ramekins and serve warm with slices of crusty baguette and butter, or keep it for another time.

If sealed with butter (see page 127), it will keep in the fridge for up to 9 days. Remove the rillettes from the fridge 30 minutes before serving to bring out the flavours.

You can also freeze the rillettes in the ramekins for up to 3 months (before sealing with butter) by wrapping each one in clingfilm/plastic wrap. If you do this, it's best to defrost them in the fridge slowly overnight before serving rather than with any heat or microwaving. You can still pour melted butter on top after defrosting, or just enjoy them without.

ROAST MARROW BUTTER WITH LEMON, PARSLEY AND CAPER OATCAKES

This is ideal served as a canapé for a drinks party or a hearty appetizer if you're following it with a lighter main dish, as the marrow is lovely and rich, like a pâté. I have paired the recipe with the zesty lemon, parsley and caper oatcakes to balance the buttery richness of the marrow topping, and it works brilliantly.

6 pieces veal or lamb marrow bone, each about 5 cm/2 inches long

20 g/1½ tablespoons butter

1 tablespoon capers, finely chopped, plus a few extra to garnish

1 teaspoon finely chopped fresh parsley

freshly squeezed juice of ½ lemon

LEMON, PARSLEY AND CAPER OATCAKES

50 g/½ cup old-fashioned rolled oats

25 g/3 tablespoons plain/all-purpose flour

20 g/1½ tablespoons butter (at room temperature)

a pinch of baking powder

finely grated zest and freshly squeezed juice of ½ lemon

1 tablespoon freshly chopped parsley

2 teaspoons capers, finely chopped

a pinch each of salt and black pepper

milk, for glazing

a 4-cm/1½-inch round fluted cookie cutter

a large baking sheet, lined with baking parchment

SERVES 4

Preheat the oven to 180°C (350°F) Gas 4.

Cover a roasting pan with kitchen foil (to catch any of the marrow that may melt out of the bones) and arrange the bones on top. Stand them up if the shape will allow you to do so.

Bake in the preheated oven for 15 minutes (no longer, to avoid melting the marrow and making it harder to scoop up – check after 10 minutes). Remove from the oven and set aside until cool enough to handle.

Melt the butter in a frying pan/skillet over a medium heat. Scoop out the roasted marrow from the bones and add it to the pan. Add the capers, parsley and a squeeze of lemon juice, and cook for 2 minutes. Spoon the mixture into a food processor and blend until smooth. Transfer to a dish or other suitable container and chill in the fridge for at least 2 hours, until just set.

While the marrow is setting, make the oatcakes. Preheat the oven to 180°C (350°F) Gas 4.

Put the oats, flour, butter, baking powder, lemon zest and juice, parsley and capers in a bowl and the salt and pepper. Rub in the butter with your fingertips until the mixture is flaky. Add a few drops of water to the mixture just to soften it enough to shape it into a ball. Lightly flour the work surface and use a rolling pin to roll out the oat mixture as you would pastry dough.

Using the cutter, stamp out rounds and arrange them on the prepared baking sheet. Bring the scraps together and re-roll to get as many oatcakes from the mixture as possible. Brush with a little milk. Bake in the preheated oven for 15 minutes, until firm. Transfer the oatcakes to a plate or cooling rack. (Tip: if you want to cool and serve the oatcakes straightaway, chill a plate in the fridge before you start and transfer the oatcakes to it to speed up the cooling time.)

Spread each oatcake with some chilled marrow butter and finish with a sprinkling of chopped capers and a squeeze of lemon juice. I like to pair these with a crisp, cool white wine such as a Pouilly Fuissé to cut through the richness of the marrow.

CHICKEN DRUMSTICK CROQUETTES

These hot and crispy croquettes are a clever way of using up the drumstick and wing meat from a chicken. Serve with a pot of sour cream on the side for dipping.

2 skinless* chicken drumsticks and 2 wings

½ white onion, finely chopped

1 teaspoon smoked paprika

a pinch of chilli/chili powder (or ½ a fresh chilli/chile, finely chopped)

1 tablespoon olive oil

salt and black pepper, to season

100 g/3½ oz. chorizo, diced

50 g/3½ tablespoons butter

190 g/1½ cups plus 1 tablespoon plain/all purpose flour

300 ml/1¼ cups milk

2 eggs, beaten

75 g/1½ cups dried breadcrumbs

300 ml/1¼ cups sunflower oil

tomato ketchup and sour-cream dip of your choice, to serve (optional)

MAKES 8

* If cooking in the US where skinless wings and drumsticks are not available, you can skin the meat after cooking or substitute boneless, skinless thighs, if preferred

Preheat the oven to 180°C (350°F) Gas 4.

Put the drumsticks and the wings in a roasting pan with the onion, paprika, chilli/chili powder and season with salt and pepper. Drizzle the olive oil over the top. Roast in the preheated oven for 30 minutes.

Meanwhile, melt the butter in a frying pan/skillet set over a medium heat. Sprinkle 140 g/1 cup plus 1 tablespoon of the flour into the pan (reserving the rest for cooking) and stir with a wooden spoon to combine and form a paste. Slowly add the milk, stirring until it's mixed in and the mixture is smooth.

Remove the pan from the heat and set aside to cool.

Once the chicken is cooked through and brown, take it out of the oven and leave until cool enough to handle.

Tear the meat off the drumstick and wing bones with your fingers and put it into a mixing bowl. Tip the cooked onions and seasoned oil from the roasting pan into the bowl and pour in the flour and butter mixture (batter). Add the chorizo and stir to combine.

Put the remaining flour (50 g/heaping ⅓ cup flour) and breadcrumbs on 2 separate plates and the eggs into a shallow bowl. Flour your hands and use them to work the chicken mixture into 8 small sausage shapes of equal size. Roll each croquette first in the flour, then in the egg and finally roll gently to coat well with the breadcrumbs.

Warm the sunflower oil into a heavy-based pan set over a medium–high heat. Meanwhile, line a large plate with paper towels.

Using metal tongs, carefully put each of the croquettes into the oil and fry for 5 minutes. Turn the croquettes over and fry for a further 5–8 minutes, until crisp and golden brown.

Serve hot with tomato ketchup and small dish of sour-cream dip on the side if liked.

HOMEMADE SCOTCH EGGS

Who doesn't love a Scotch egg? This British classic has enjoyed a revival in recent years and is surprisingly simple to make at home. They are a fun choice for entertaining too – served warm with a soft yolk middle and accompanied with some well-dressed salad leaves, they make the perfect appetizer or light lunch.

8 eggs

600 g/21 oz. really good pork mince/ground pork (see page 27 for hand-mincing/hand-cutting)

30 g/2 tablespoons tomato purée/paste

1 garlic clove, finely chopped

1 teaspoon freshly chopped parsley

1 tablespoon freshly chopped chives

½ teaspoon mustard powder

20 g/1½ tablespoons plain/all-purpose flour, plus extra for sprinkling

1.5 litres/6 cups vegetable oil

200 g/2½ cups dried breadcrumbs

salt and black pepper, to season

lemon wedges and mixed salad leaves or pickle of your choice, to serve (optional)

MAKES 6

Bring a large pan of water to the boil. Using a slotted spoon, lower 6 of the eggs into the water. Boil for 5 minutes for softer centres, 8 minutes for hard-boiled/hard-cooked eggs.

Meanwhile, put the minced/ground pork in a mixing bowl. Add the tomato purée/paste, garlic, parsley, chives and mustard powder and mix to combine. Season with salt and pepper.

Lightly flour a work surface or board. Flour your hands and use them to break the pork mixture into six pieces of equal size, roll them into balls and then flatten them on the surface with the heel of your hand to make round patties. These need to be big enough to fold around the whole eggs.

Remove the boiled eggs from the water. Drop them into a bowl of cold water. When they are cool enough to handle, peel off the shells.

Pour the vegetable oil into a heavy-based pan and warm over a medium–high heat. Meanwhile, line a large plate with paper towels.

Put each peeled egg in the middle of a pork patty, then fold the patty around the egg, using your fingers to move and squeeze the pork around the egg until it is completely sealed inside.

Put the flour and breadcrumbs on separate plates. Beat the remaining 2 eggs and pour into a shallow bowl. Roll each pork ball first in the flour, then roll in the beaten egg and finally roll gently to coat with the breadcrumbs.

Using metal tongs, carefully put two of the balls into the hot oil and deep-fry for 15 minutes, until crisp and golden brown. Remove each ball from the oil and transfer to the paper-towel-lined plate to drain. Repeat with the remaining Scotch eggs.

Serve warm with a wedge of lemon for squeezing and mixed salad leaves. Alternatively, chill and enjoy as a cold cut with pickles.

The Scotch eggs will keep in the fridge for up to 1 week and should be stored in an airtight container.

BEEF CARPACCIO WITH ROCKET AND PARMESAN SALAD

This recipe celebrates beef fillet/tenderloin as does the Flash Fillet Roast on page 153. Because we're serving it almost raw here you get a very different but equally fantastic eating experience. If you're cutting your own fillet/tenderloin, the middle section is best for Beef Wellington (see page 154) or fillet steaks but here, the tail end works well. It takes up to seven days to prepare, so do plan ahead!

a 800-g/1¾-lb. piece of beef fillet/tenderloin (allow about 200 g/7 oz. per person)

1 tablespoon olive oil

about 100 g/3 cups wild rocket/arugula

80 g/3 oz. Parmesan cheese, shaved

extra virgin olive oil, to drizzle

salt and black pepper, to season

a 20-cm/8-inch square piece of muslin/cheesecloth or cotton

kitchen twine

SERVES 4

The real trick to carpaccio is to get the piece of beef as dry as possible before preparing it. You will be searing the outside of the meat, so don't worry about hanging it for a couple of days beforehand to help it dry (see Note on page 137 about serving rare beef).

Wrap the piece of beef in the muslin/cheesecloth and secure with twine. Suspend it by tying it to a shelf in your fridge. To do this, pull out your fridge shelf so you can tie the twine around the back and tighten to lift the meat into the air underneath. Ideally you should leave it for at least 2–3 days (and up to 4 days) but even a few hours of this will help the result if you don't have more time available.

When you are ready to serve, remove the beef from the fridge, unwrap it and discard the muslin/cheesecloth and twine.

Heat the olive oil over a medium–high heat in a heavy-based frying pan/skillet until it bubbles.

Add a pinch of salt to the pan then lift the beef into the pan and sear it by rolling it in the hot oil, just a few seconds on each side, but ensuring that the heat has made contact with the entire surface of the meat.

Remove from the pan and transfer to a board. Using a very sharp knife, slice it as thinly as possible.

Put a few slices of carpaccio on each serving plate and drop a handful of rocket/arugula on top. Scatter with some Parmesan shavings, add a crack of black pepper and a drizzle of a good fruity olive oil. Serve immediately.

STEAK TARTARE

Use the best-quality meat you can find to get the most out of this classic French dish made with raw beef. And if you are worried about food safety, let me reassure you. This recipe requires 350 g/¾ lb. of beef, but you'll only in fact be eating around 200 g/7 oz. of it and this will be the meat at the centre of the piece. You're going to mix it with the other ingredients and enjoy it straightaway, before any bacteria has a chance to make contact with it, let alone contaminate it. It is only contact with the air that carries the bacteria that will spoil perishable foods. What you trim off won't be wasted either. It will be fresh for a few more days, ideal to use in a stir fry, and once cooked, any bacteria will have been killed. It's a refreshing and sophisticated plate and well worth trying if you've not done so before.

40 g/⅓ cup very finely diced red onion

1 gherkin/pickle or 4 small cornichons, finely diced

2 teaspoons capers, crushed or finely chopped

½ garlic clove, finely chopped (optional)

1 teaspoon tomato purée/paste

5–6 drops Tabasco (or other hot pepper sauce), to taste

2 teaspoons Worcestershire sauce

1 teaspoon finely chopped fresh parsley

350 g/¾ lb. beef, ideally fillet/tenderloin or trimmed sirloin

1 very fresh egg (optional)

salt and black pepper

snipped chives, to garnish

horseradish, to serve

SERVES 1

First wash your hands in hot water with plenty of soap. Also wash a chopping board, mixing bowl, sharp knife and serving plate really thoroughly in piping hot water and washing liquid and dry with a clean kitchen cloth.

Put the onion, gherkin, capers, garlic (if using), tomato purée/paste, Tabasco, Worcestershire sauce and parsley in a mixing bowl and stir to combine. Set aside.

Using the knife, cut thin strips off the beef, from all around the edge of the piece of meat and set aside (see recipe introduction). Then chop the remaining meat from the centre into tiny pieces, aiming to get it as close to mince/ground meat in appearance as you can.

Tip the beef into the mixing bowl with the other ingredients and mix really well, using your hands to rub flavour into the meat so it is seasoned and tender. Check the seasoning and add salt, pepper and more Tabasco to taste.

Spoon the mixture directly onto a serving plate. Press down with your thumb to make an indentation in the middle. Crack and separate the egg and drop the yolk only into the dent. Add a spoonful of horseradish to the side, grind a little black pepper over the top, sprinkle with chives and serve immediately.

POACHED WHOLE BALLOTINE CHICKEN WITH BASIL PESTO

Ballotine is a French term for a boned, stuffed and poached piece of poultry, from the word '*balle*' meaning 'a package of goods'. The description is now sometimes used to refer to other stuffed meat joints like lamb and pork but, staying true to the traditional recipe, we're going to use chicken here. Chilled leftovers (known as '*galantine*', which refers to poached, chilled and sliced meat) can be used to make a delicious sandwich. Split and butter a soft, oaty wholemeal/whole-wheat roll, add slices of the ballotine, some goat's cheese, sun-blush tomatoes and lettuce.

1 boned*, whole, free-range chicken (weighing about 2 kg/4½ lbs.)

braised red cabbage and Fancy Mashed Potatoes (see page 233), to serve (optional)

BASIL PESTO

50 g/scant ½ cup pine nuts

12–15 large fresh basil leaves

2 garlic cloves

50 ml/3½ tablespoons extra virgin olive oil

60 g/1 cup finely grated fresh Parmesan cheese

freshly squeezed lemon juice

salt and black pepper, to season

butchers' string or kitchen twine (optional)

SERVES 6–8

* If you're cutting your own whole chicken, see page 70 for instructions on how to debone

To make the pesto, heat a small frying pan/skillet without oil and dry-fry the pine nuts for 2–3 minutes until brown and lightly toasted. Watch the pan closely, as they can quickly catch and burn. Remove the pan from the heat and let cool.

Tip the cooled pine nuts into a food processor and add the basil and garlic. Season with salt and pepper.

Whizz the ingredients, whilst slowly adding the olive oil so it blends in a little at a time. Add the Parmesan and a little lemon juice and blend until smooth.

Transfer the pesto into a small dish (a rubber spatula is helpful for scraping around the bowl of the food processor to get it all out). Check the seasoning and add more salt and pepper to taste. Use your hands to rub the pesto all around the inside of the boneless chicken. Make sure you coat as much of the surface as you can, getting into all the nooks.

Next, roll the bird up tightly. Use the butchers' string method on page 26 to roll it and then wrap in clingfilm/plastic wrap. Alternatively you can wrap it tightly in clingfilm/plastic wrap without tying it, which will still work okay. Wrap it securely in kitchen foil.

Fill a large lidded pan with water (to match the height of the wrapped bird; it doesn't need to cover it) and bring just to the boil.

Carefully lower the foil-covered parcel into the water and simmer over a low heat for 35 minutes, until poached. Be careful not to let the water boil around it, as the chicken will dry out if it's too hot.

Remove the parcel from the water and leave to rest in the foil for 10 minutes before unwrapping and transferring to a board or plate. Carve into slices straight away and serve hot with red cabbage and fancy mashed potatoes, if liked, or chill to eat cold.

DUCK, VENISON AND HALLOUMI SKEWERS

Duck and venison are often used in recipes that combine sweet and savoury flavours. Here, a delightfully rich, fruity marinade prepares these skewers for grilling or barbecuing.

2 tablespoons olive oil

1 tablespoon Cointreau (or other orange-flavoured liquor)

2 teaspoons soft/light brown sugar

1 red onion, finely chopped

2 teaspoons finely chopped fresh flat-leaf parsley, plus extra to garnish

a 400-g/14-oz. venison loin, trimmed

1 boneless duck breast, skin on

200 g/7 oz. halloumi (a semi-hard, unripened, brined cheese from Cyprus) or similar

6 fresh plums, halved and stoned/pitted

salt and black pepper, to season

lime wedges, to serve

6 stainless steel or wooden skewers (soak wooden skewers in water before use to prevent them from burning)

MAKES 6

To prepare the marinade, combine the olive oil, Cointreau, sugar, red onion and parsley in a small bowl, season with salt and pepper and mix well.

Cut the venison and duck into chunks of equal size. Keep the skin on the duck at this stage. You can remove it later when you come to assemble the skewers, but as the venison and the duck look very similar after marinating, leaving the skin on will help you tell them apart and distribute the meats evenly along the skewers.

Transfer the marinade to a sealable bag or a bowl suitable for marinating. Add the duck and venison to the bag or bowl and shake or toss to coat the meats really well with the marinade. Seal the bag or cover the bowl with clingfilm/plastic wrap. Put in the fridge and chill for at least 1 hour.

Cut the halloumi into pieces the same size as the chunks of meat. Remove the meats from the marinade (reserving the marinade). Thread the marinaded meats, halloumi cubes and plum halves alternately on the skewers (aiming for 2–3 pieces of each on a single skewer).

Brush, spoon or rub the reserved marinade over the skewers.

These can be cooked by a number of methods. You can grill them over a preheated charcoal or gas barbecue, on the stovetop in a very hot ridged griddle pan/skillet, turning every minute. Or lastly, under a preheated grill/broiler for about 15 minutes, turning them a couple of times. (It's advisable to line the grill/broiler pan with foil to catch the juices.)

Scatter over some chopped flat-leaf parsley and serve hot with wedges of lime for squeezing (which just sharpens and balances the rich sweetness of the flavours).

PHEASANT AND GAMMON PIE

Like a lot of game, pheasant is delicious when paired with sweet and salty flavours, so the addition of gammon and cranberries here is a winner. This is a brilliant way to make use of any leftover Glazed Roast Gammon (see page 211).

2 tablespoons olive oil

1 red onion, diced

1 leek, split lengthways, rinsed and thinly sliced

1 garlic clove, chopped

600 g/21 oz. boneless pheasant, diced

a handful of fresh or frozen cranberries

1 teaspoon soft brown sugar

a handful of roughly chopped fresh flat-leaf parsley

20 g/2⅓ tablespoons plain/all-purpose flour

100 ml/⅓ cup white wine

150 ml/⅔ cup White or Brown Chicken Stock (see page 32)

150 ml/⅔ cup double/heavy cream

salt and black pepper, to season

200–300 g/7–10½ oz. cooked gammon, bacon or ham, diced

Fancy Mashed Potatoes (see page 217) and steamed vegetables, to serve

PASTRY

200 g/1½ cups plain/all-purpose flour, plus extra for sprinkling

100 g/7 tablespoons butter, at room temperature, plus a little extra for greasing

1–2 teaspoons finely chopped fresh tarragon (optional)

1 egg, beaten

a 25–30-cm/9¾–12-inch deep pie dish

a pie funnel (optional)

SERVES 4

Heat the oil in a large frying pan/skillet and add the onion, leek and garlic. Gently sauté until soft and translucent.

Add the pheasant to the pan and cook for 4–5 minutes over a medium heat, until browned.

Add the cranberries, sugar and parsley, season with salt and pepper and stir well to mix. Sprinkle the flour over the top and wait for it to take on colour, then stir it in.

Pour the white wine and stock into the pan, increase the heat and bring the mixture to the boil. Add the cream, bring back to boil, then reduce the heat to a simmer. Add the gammon and cook for 15 minutes.

Meanwhile preheat the oven to 180°C (350°F) Gas 4.

To make the pastry, put the flour in a mixing bowl and add the butter. Rub the butter into the flour using your fingertips. Add the tarragon, if using, and a pinch of salt and then 3–4 tablespoons of cold water, 1 tablespoon at a time. Use your hands to bring the dough together into a ball.

Lightly dust a work surface with flour. Use a rolling pin to roll out the dough to a size sufficient to generously cover your pie dish. Use your finger to run butter around the top 2 cm/¾ inch outside edge of the pie dish. If you have a pie funnel, put this in the centre of the dish. (This enables the steam to escape and thus keeps the filling thick and the pastry crisp.)

Pour the filling mixture into the pie dish/pan. Lift up the pastry and place it on the top of the filling. Use a sharp knife to cut a small cross in the centre of the pastry lid (directly on top of the pie funnel, if using). Trim the edges or let them overhang, as preferred, and press around the edge to seal it to the sides of the dish.

Using a pastry brush, glaze the top of the pie with the beaten egg. Transfer the dish to a baking sheet to catch any escaping filling and bake in the preheated oven for 30–40 minutes, until the top is golden brown and crisp.

Serve hot with mashed potatoes and a steamed vegetable, such as green beans or broccoli, if liked.

RABBIT AND SEAFOOD PAELLA

What most people know as a Spanish paella (and what is offered in restaurants all over Spain) is a chicken and seafood rice dish. But in some regions of Spain rice dishes featuring rabbit are more commonplace and include hunter's rice (rich with foraged mushrooms) like Valencian paella, which includes rabbit as well as chicken. I have found that the oakier, darker meat of rabbit works well with cured meats, so my recipe pairs it with chorizo and bacon as well as seafood, with delicious results.

1 tablespoon olive oil

10 g/2 teaspoons butter

1 red onion, finely chopped

2–3 spring onions/scallions, chopped

2 garlic cloves, finely chopped

1 fresh red chilli/chile, deseeded and finely chopped

120 g/¼ lb. rabbit meat, diced

100 g/3½ oz streaky/fatty bacon, chopped

100 g/3½ oz. chorizo, diced

1 red (bell) pepper, diced

80 g/¾ cup peeled raw prawns/shrimp

4–6 raw scallops

100 ml/⅓ cup plus 1 tablespoon white wine

2 tablespoons frozen peas

1–2 teaspoons smoked Spanish paprika (pimentón)

3–4 saffron strands, ground or 1 teaspoon ground saffron

80 ml/⅓ cup White or Brown Chicken Stock (see page 32, or made from a stock cube)

150 g/¾ cup short-grain rice (such as Arborio or Calasparra)

1 tablespoon chopped fresh flat-leaf parsley

salt and black pepper, to taste

sour cream (optional) and lemon wedges, to serve

SERVES 2

Heat the oil and butter in a large frying pan/skillet set over a moderate heat. Add the onion and spring onions/scallions and fry for 2 minutes. Add the garlic and fresh chilli/chile to the pan and fry for a further 1 minute or so, until the onions are soft and browning.

Add the rabbit, bacon and chorizo to the pan and fry over a medium heat for 8–9 minutes, until the rabbit is golden brown.

Add the red (bell) pepper, prawns/shrimp and scallops to the pan and cook, stirring for 4–5 minutes.

Add the peas, paprika and saffron to the pan and stir.

Pour the white wine and chicken stock into the pan, stir well, and increase the heat to bring the liquid to the boil.

Once boiling, tip in the rice, reduce the heat and simmer, uncovered and stirring occasionally, for 20 minutes, or until the rice is soft and 'al dente' to the bite. (If the paella starts to dry and catch on the bottom of the pan, just add a little more stock or water and stir.)

Taste and add salt and pepper to taste, sprinkle with parsley and serve straight away with sour cream on the side (if using) and lemon wedges for squeezing.

LAMB KLEFTIKO WITH SPICED YOGURT

Kleftiko is one of the most popular Greek dishes. Lamb is seasoned with rosemary, garlic and lemon, and slow-roasted with potatoes in a sealed earthenware pot, but it can be cooked at home in a paper parcel with equally delicious results.

6 garlic cloves

finely grated zest and juice of 1 lemon

2 tablespoons fresh oregano leaves, chopped

½ teaspoon ground cinnamon

¼ teaspoon ground nutmeg

¼ teaspoon mustard powder

3 tablespoons olive oil

a 2-kg/3½-lbs. leg of lamb, bone in

1 kg/2¼ lbs. waxy potatoes, peeled and quartered

2 sprigs fresh rosemary

3 bay leaves

salt and black pepper, to season

SPICED YOGURT

2 fresh red chillies/chiles, deseeded

1 garlic clove, crushed

1 tablespoon each of chopped fresh flat-leaf parsley, chives and coriander/cilantro

2–3 fresh mint leaves

½ teaspoon ground cumin

200 ml/¾ cup natural/plain Greek yogurt

SERVES 6

Preheat the oven to 180°C (350°F) Gas 4.

With their skins still on, flatten the garlic cloves with the side of a knife. Put them on a baking sheet and roast in the preheated oven for 20 minutes.

Put the lemon zest and juice in a small bowl with the oregano, cinnamon, nutmeg, mustard powder and half of the olive oil. Add a pinch each of salt and pepper and whisk with a fork to combine.

Remove the garlic cloves from the oven and, once cool enough to handle, squeeze out the roasted soft centre and discard the skins.

Using a sharp knife, score lines across the outer surface of the lamb and rub the garlic cloves and then the lemon and herb mixture into the lines and coat the outside.

Put a large sheet of baking parchment on a roasting pan that will fit on a shelf in your fridge. Place the lamb leg on top. Wrap the paper tightly and then wrap the whole thing in clingfilm/plastic wrap. Transfer to the fridge for at least 1 hour or ideally overnight.

When you are ready to cook the lamb, preheat the oven to 160°C (325°F) Gas 3.

Toss the peeled potatoes in rest of the olive oil and season with salt and pepper.

Lay a large sheet of foil on a baking sheet, enough to fold right over the potatoes and the lamb leg. Remove the clingfilm/plastic wrap from the lamb and put it (still wrapped in its baking parchment) on top of the foil; open out the baking parchment.

Move the joint to the side and pop the seasoned potatoes in the bottom of the parcel. Add the sprigs of rosemary and the bay leaves and then place the joint of lamb on top. Transfer to the preheated oven. After 20 minutes of cooking time, fold the baking parchment and the foil over the top tightly and return to the oven for 2½–3 hours. Then pull out the oven shelf, carefully open out the foil and baking parchment and baste the joint with the cooking juices. Increase the heat to 200°C (400°F) Gas 6 and return to the oven for about 10 minutes. This will brown the lamb and crisp the potatoes.

To make the spiced yogurt, whizz all the ingredients except the yogurt in a food processor. Scoop out and mix with the yogurt. Serve chilled with slices of the hot lamb and the potatoes.

MARINATED LAMB STEAKS

For some reason, lamb rump or leg steaks are not as popular as beef steaks – they just don't seem to be an obvious choice for a cut of lamb. However, I think they're terrific, especially when marinated, and they are so easy to cook and eat.

This recipe is inspired by Moroccan flavourings, but you can substitute a sweet redcurrant marinade, or use the kleftiko marinade (see left) here, adding the rosemary and bay leaves to the marinating liquid. If you're cutting your own lamb leg, this is an especially easy part to extract, see pages 53–55.

2 tablespoons olive oil (or argan oil, if available), plus extra for cooking

1 teaspoon paprika

½ teaspoon cayenne pepper

1 tablespoon ground cumin

½ teaspoon whole pink or black peppercorns

2 trimmed lamb rump/leg steaks (usually 200 g/7 oz. each)

2 tablespoons of chopped fresh flat-leaf parsley, to garnish

a generous pinch of salt

TO SERVE

plain couscous

a pinch of saffron threads or 1 teaspoon ground saffron

salad of peeled and sliced orange segments and pitted/stoned black olives (optional)

SERVES 2

Start this recipe the day before you want to serve it.

Combine the olive oil, paprika, cayenne pepper, cumin and peppercorns in a bowl and add the salt. Whisk the mixture with a fork to combine.

Pour into a sealable bag or suitable container and add the steaks. Shake the bag or spoon the marinade over the meat to cover. Put in the fridge and leave to marinate overnight.

When ready to serve, prepare sufficient couscous for 2 servings according the instructions on the packet, adding the saffron to the liquid you are using, usually water or vegetable stock, as preferred. Cover and set aside until needed.

Warm a ridged griddle/grill pan (or heavy frying pan/skillet) over a high heat and add a drop of olive oil. Remove the steaks from the bag or container and reserve the marinade.

When the pan is very hot, add the steaks and sear for just 20 seconds on each side, using tongs to gently turn the meat over.

Reduce the heat and pour the reserved marinade over the steaks. Cook for a further 2 minutes on either side for medium-rare or 3–4 minutes for medium-well done.

Sprinkle with chopped parsley and serve straight away with spoonfuls of saffron couscous and a simple Moroccan-style orange and olive salad on the side, if liked.

APPLE, PLUM AND CINNAMON LAMB TAGINE

Inspired by a Belvoir fruit cordial we were served on a break during the lamb cutting section of a butchery course... I thought I'd try the combination for a type of tagine! If you're cutting your leg of lamb, this recipe is perfect for the rump/chump top meat. Just trim it and cut into 2-cm/1-inch dice.

20 g/1 tablespoon butter

800 g–1 kg/1¾–2 lbs. lamb, diced

6 small shallots, peeled and halved

4 fresh plums, peeled, stoned/pitted and quartered

1 small cooking apple, peeled, cored and diced

1 teaspoon finely chopped fresh sage

1 teaspoon ground cinnamon

2 teaspoons dark brown sugar

200 ml/⅔ cup Brown Chicken Stock (see page 32) or a chicken stock cube dissolved in 200 ml/⅔ cup boiling water

couscous, to serve

freshly chopped flat-leaf parsley, to garnish

salt and black pepper, to season

SERVES 4

Preheat the oven to 160°C (325°F) Gas 3.

Set a large lidded heatproof casserole dish on the stovetop over a medium heat. Add the butter, lamb and the shallots to the casserole and fry for 6–8 minutes until the lamb is browned, stirring often. Add the plums, apple, sage, cinnamon, sugar and stock.

Bring to the boil then reduce the heat and simmer for 5–10 minutes. Place the lid on the casserole and transfer it to the preheated oven. Cook for 2 hours, until the meat is tender and the sauce rich and sticky.

Meanwhile, prepare enough couscous for 4 servings according to the instructions on the packet.

Remove the tagine from the oven, taste and adjust the seasoning with salt and pepper.

Serve hot, spooned over a bed of couscous and sprinkled with chopped parsley.

KOREAN-STYLE BUTTERFLIED LAMB

This butterflied lamb joint is marinated in Asian flavourings ahead of cooking. It looks really impressive (and smells just as good!), so is perfect for entertaining a larger number of people. It's an easy idea for a barbecue/cook out, too, as you produce a big piece of boneless, really flavoursome meat, which is easy to carve up and tuck into. The joint needs to be marinated overnight, so start preparing the recipe the day before you intend to cook it.

1 butterflied lamb joint (see pages 53–55 for cutting your own lamb leg)

MARINADE

3 tablespoons sesame oil

3 garlic cloves, chopped

4 spring onions/scallions, roughly chopped

a 2-cm/1-inch piece of fresh ginger, peeled and chopped or 1 teaspoon ground ginger

2 tablespoons soy sauce

2 tablespoons mirin (Japanese rice wine)

1 tablespoon tomato purée/paste

1 teaspoon miso paste (optional)

½ teaspoon mustard powder

a generous pinch each of salt and black pepper

SERVES 6–8

The day before you plan to cook the joint, prepare the marinade. Put the oil, garlic, spring onions/scallions, ginger, soy sauce, mirin, tomato purée/paste and miso paste (if using) in a food processor and add a generous pinch each of salt and black pepper. Whizz until combined.

Lay the joint out flat on a clean work surface or baking sheet. Remove the marinade from the food processor using a spatula and rub it all over the meat, using your fingers to push it into every join and dip in the meat. Reserve any leftover marinade for later.

Fold the joint back up and put it into a large sealable bag or suitable container. Pour the rest of the marinade into the bag or container and seal. Transfer to the fridge and leave overnight.

The following day, take the joint out of the fridge and remove it from its marinade. You can cook it on a barbecue/outdoor grill, on the stovetop or under the grill/broiler.

To cook on the barbecue/outdoor grill, put the joint on the hottest part of the grill and cook for 3 minutes on either side. Move the meat away from the heat and cover with the lid. Cook for 8–10 minutes on either side then place it back over the hottest part for a few minutes to make it crisp before serving.

Indoors, a large enough griddle/grill pan will do the job. Heat the pan to a medium heat. Cover the main part of the joint with foil so that it doesn't char and cooks through properly, cook for 10 minutes on each side then remove the foil, increase the heat to high and cook for 8–10 minutes on either side to crisp up the surface.

Alternatively, cook it under a preheated grill/broiler. Preheat to medium and cook the joint on the middle shelf for 25 minutes, turning halfway through cooking time until it's starting to crisp on the outside. Turn the grill/broiler up to the highest setting and cook for a further 5–6 minutes on either side.

To serve, either slice from it flat or, for a bit of theatre, fold the meat back to its original shape, roll it with your utensils (it'll be too hot to handle yet), stick a meat fork through the middle to lift it to a board and then slice like a roasting joint so it falls into juicy pieces.

FLASH FILLET ROAST WITH MUSTARD SAUCE

The joy of a fillet/tenderloin is that, as the name suggests, it is so tender it is the perfect choice for serving rare or, indeed, raw as in Steak Tartare (page 137).

If you're cutting your own fillet, this is a great way to use the thinnest end, including the tail. We're only flash-roasting here, so we don't have to worry about balancing the cooking time of the different thicknesses of meat. I would go for about 200 g/7 oz. of meat per person. Start with more than you think, because you can always cut a steak off the thicker end for another time, which is better than starting with a piece that is too small for the number of you eating, and having to cook a lonely steak on the side to make up for it!

an 800-g/1¾-lbs. piece of beef fillet/tenderloin (allow about 200 g/7 oz. per person)

20 g/1½ tablespoons butter

salt and black pepper, to rub

Buttery Crushed Potatoes (see page 217), cooked spinach and greens, to serve

MUSTARD SAUCE

1 garlic clove, finely chopped

½ teaspoon Dijon mustard

1–2 tablespoons crème fraîche or sour cream

SERVES 4

Preheat the oven to 200°C (400°F) Gas 6.

Take the beef and rub some salt, pepper and half the butter all over it.

Heat a frying pan/skillet with the other half of the butter over a high heat, so that it is completely hot and the butter starts to brown. Put the piece of fillet/tenderloin in the frying pan/skillet and roll it over every 5 seconds, lightly pressing on the top for each side. You need to sear the whole surface, but just the surface rather than cooking it through. Use tongs to hold it upright to sear the ends too.

Transfer the meat to a roasting pan (do not wash the frying pan/skillet yet) and cook in the hot oven for 15 minutes.

Once the meat is cooked, remove it from the oven and set it aside to rest for a few minutes while you make the sauce.

Put the same frying pan/skillet you used to cook the meat over a low heat and throw the garlic in to brown. Add the Dijon mustard and crème fraîche and stir. Keep over the heat while you slice the meat for serving.

Serve the fillet/tenderloin with the sauce. This is great with buttery crushed potatoes, some baby spinach and other greens.

BEEF WELLINGTON

This is a classic dinner party dish that, when executed perfectly, will never fail to impress your guests. Fillet/tenderloin is an expensive cut of beef, so this dish should be reserved for special occasions.

50 g/3½ tablespoons butter

salt, to season

1 kg/2 lbs. trimmed beef fillet/tenderloin (ask for an even cut from the middle)

1 garlic clove, finely chopped

3 shallots, finely chopped

100 g/3½ oz. button/white mushrooms, finely chopped

40 g/1½ oz. lamb's liver, finely diced

1 teaspoon Dijon mustard

4 tablespoons tomato purée/paste

a pinch of freshly chopped thyme

a pinch of freshly chopped parsley

salad and steamed new potatoes, to serve (optional)

PASTRY

150 g/⅔ cup butter

325 g/scant 2½ cups plain/all-purpose flour, plus extra for dusting

1–2 tablespoons cold water

salt and black pepper

1 egg, beaten

SERVES 4

Take the butter out of the fridge for at least 20 minutes in advance to soften a little.

Heat a frying pan/skillet with a little of the butter and a sprinkle of salt. Sear the piece of fillet/tenderloin for just a minute, rolling it constantly to brown the whole surface and use tongs to hold it upright to sear the ends too. Remove and set on a plate to cool.

In the same pan, add the rest of the butter to fry the chopped garlic, shallots, mushrooms, liver, mustard, tomato purée/paste, thyme and parsley. Add some salt and pepper and fry until nice and soft – the more finely the shallots and mushrooms are chopped the better, so that it becomes more like paté. Remove from the heat.

To make the pastry, rub the butter, flour and a pinch of salt together with your fingertips until the mixture resembles breadcrumbs. Add the cold water, a tablespoonful at a time, until you can combine the crumbled mixture into a ball of pastry. Don't add too much water.

Sprinkle some flour on a surface and roll out three-quarters of the pastry into a large square; try to keep it to 5 mm/¼ inch thick and as even as possible. At this stage, lift the pastry square onto a piece of baking parchment so that it's easier to transfer to the baking sheet later. Spread the mushroom mixture over three-quarters of the pastry, leaving the top quarter uncoated.

Roll the remaining pastry out to the same thickness as before and trim lengths 5 mm/¼ inch wide. Cut half of these in half.

Preheat the oven to 170°C (325°F) Gas 3.

Place the seared fillet/tenderloin across the top of the coated area and fold over the pastry so as much of the meat is covered with the mushroom mixture as possible. Brush a little of the beaten egg along the top and fold the uncoated quarter of pastry over so it's wrapped like a parcel. Smudge down the join of the pastry with your fingertips to help it stick across the top. Pinch together the ends to seal as well. Brush the rest of the beaten egg over the top of the pastry then lay the long strips of trimmed pastry over the top. Weave the shorter lengths beneath these and glaze.

Lift the baking parchment onto a baking sheet and place in the oven on the middle shelf. Roast for 45 minutes, until the pastry is browned and cooked. Let stand for 10 minutes before serving.

OSSO BUCCO

Italian for 'bone with a hole', osso bucco is named after the cross-cut veal shin/shank from which it is made. The emphasis is on the flavour the cut has from being attached to the bone and from its delicious marrow. Veal is excellent for this recipe because the bone and marrow are still young and soft; if you did this with a beef shin, you would have lovely soft meat from the slow-cooking but not nearly as much of the rich flavour in the sauce from the bone and marrow.

2 pieces of veal shin/shank, about 4 cm/1¾ inches thick

1 tablespoon plain/all-purpose flour

30 g/2 tablespoons butter

1 white onion, chopped

2 garlic cloves

finely grated zest of ½ lemon

4 teaspoons tomato purée/paste

100 g/3¾ oz. drained canned chopped tomatoes or 1 fresh beef/beefsteak tomato, deseeded and chopped

a pinch of freshly chopped sage

a pinch of freshly chopped basil

80 g/1¼ cups chopped mushrooms (optional)

200 ml/scant 1 cup white wine

200 ml/scant 1 cup White or Brown Chicken Stock (see page 32)

salt and pepper, to season

saffron rice, to serve

SERVES 2

Coat the pieces of veal shin/shank in the flour. Heat half the butter in a pan over a medium heat and brown the coated meat for 1 minute on either side. Remove the meat pieces and set aside.

In the same pan, add a the rest of the butter and fry the onion and garlic over a high heat for 5–6 minutes, until softened.

Add the lemon zest, tomato purée/paste, chopped tomatoes, sage, basil, mushrooms, if using, and some salt and pepper. Give it a stir and then pour over the wine and stock.

Bring to the boil, then reduce the heat to a low simmer. Lift the veal pieces back into the sauce and turn them over a couple of times to coat. Put a lid half over the top of the pan and leave to cook over a low heat for 1 hour.

You want the sauce to darken and go sticky. If it's still light after an hour, remove the lid, increase the heat and cook until the sauce thickens a little. Serve on saffron rice.

VEAL INVOLTINI

Whereas the Osso Bucco (opposite) really needs to be made with veal, this recipe works well when made with beef, too – some lean topside/top round, really flattened with a tenderizer/pounded thin, is lovely and cooks just as well as veal. It's an impressive-sounding dinner party main course, but it is actually quite simple to make: quick and fresh when you have guests coming for lunch on a warm summer's day.

4–6 pieces of tenderized/thinly pounded veal loin or beef topside/top rump, about 8 cm/ 3½ inches long and 4 cm/ 1¾ inches wide

a small handful of freshly chopped basil

a small handful of freshly chopped parsley

4–6 slices of prosciutto

4–6 anchovy fillets

4–6 slices of Parmesan cheese

3 tablespoons olive oil

crusty bread or Foolproof Roasties (see page 200), to serve (optional)

TOMATO SAUCE

3 tablespoons olive oil

2 beef/beefsteak tomatoes, chopped

1 red onion, diced

1 garlic clove

1 tablespoon red wine vinegar

salt and black pepper, to season

SERVES 2

Start by making the tomato sauce. Heat the olive oil in a pan and fry the tomatoes, onion, garlic, red wine vinegar and some seasoning lightly for a few minutes – you want to keep a little crunch, as this should be more like a hot salsa than a smooth sauce.

Meanwhile, take one piece of the meat at a time. Sprinkle a little of the basil and parsley on the top and season with salt and pepper

Lay a prosciutto slice flat on a surface, and then top with an anchovy fillet, a slice of Parmesan and a piece of veal. Roll up the meat and use a cocktail stick/toothpick to hold the join of the meat together. (Don't let the fold come too far back around the rolled piece or it will take too long to cook through the double layer of meat. Aim for a crossover of about 2.5 cm/1 inch at the join and trim the rest of the meat away.) Repeat with the remaining ingredients to make 4–6 rolls.

Heat the olive oil in another pan over a medium heat and fry the involtini for 8–10 minutes, turning often to ensure even cooking.

Add the tomato sauce and a little more seasoning to taste and then reduce the heat to a simmer. Cook for 10 minutes, until the veal is cooked through.

Serve just as they are with some crusty bread for a light lunch or with some herby foolproof roasties for a fuller meal. A glass of Chianti will complete the Italian spread!

LONG AND SLOW

COQ AU VIN

Some of my favourite meat dishes were once considered to be a 'poor man's' meal and often they used an abundance of seasonings to help to disguise cheaper meats or so-called 'lesser' cuts. In fact, they actually celebrate the flavours and combinations that work amazingly with good meat. They're often not difficult to make, and the meat will collapse off the bone or dissolve in your mouth. This recipe still takes a little time in the oven but it's a simpler approach with fewer stages than are sometimes traditionally involved. Serve with rice for a heartier meal.

1 whole jointed chicken (see pages 69–71), or 2 thighs, 2 drumsticks and 2 breasts

250 ml/1 cup red wine

3 bay leaves

2 garlic cloves

3 tablespoons olive oil

45 g/3 tablespoons butter

salt and black pepper, to season

75 g/generous 1 cup chopped mushrooms

6 shallots, chopped

85 g/3 oz. pancetta, diced

2 tablespoons plain/all-purpose flour

400 ml/1⅔ White Chicken Stock (see page 32)

freshly squeezed juice of ½ lemon

green beans, to serve

SERVES 4

Keep the thighs and drumsticks on the bone but debone the breast joint and cut it into smaller thirds. I don't use the wings in this recipe as they can be a bit fiddly to debone before serving so cover and refrigerate to cook at another time.

Put the chicken in a bowl or sandwich bag with the red wine, bay leaves, chopped garlic and 1 tablespoon of the olive oil. Seal the bag or cover the bowl and leave in the fridge to marinate for at least 1 hour, or ideally overnight.

Preheat the oven to 160°C (325°F) Gas 3.

Heat half the butter in a large, deep frying pan/skillet and fry the salt, pepper, pancetta, shallots and mushrooms over a high heat for about 5 minutes, until the pancetta browns.

Take the chicken pieces out of the bag or bowl, leaving the marinade in there for the moment, and add the chicken pieces to the mushrooms, shallots and pancetta for a few minutes, until they are sealed all over.

Add the marinade from the bag or bowl and stir well. Sprinkle the flour over the top and undisturbed there for a minute to absorb the flavours, then stir in.

Add the stock and lemon juice. Mix well and then transfer the contents to a casserole dish. Cover with a lid (or with foil) and cook in the preheated oven for 1½ hours.

If you want to remove the bones, remove the thighs and drumsticks and carefully pinch them to remove the bones – make sure you find the fibula bone on both drumsticks (the very thin, needle like bone). Return the meat to the casserole and use a fork to break the tender chicken chunks into shreds. Mix together. Alternatively, leave the meat on the bone and serve in whole pieces.

Serve with green beans or with rice for a fuller meal. A crisp dry white wine or cider is lovely with this.

PORK AND BOSTON BEANS

Inspired by an American adopted by London, who came to a bacon-making course we once ran, I thought I'd have a crack at some Boston Baked Beans. Hoping just to do it justice, I had not anticipated the joy of making my own baked beans and will never be able to go back to flavourless canned ones again! Whether you use good-quality pork sausages or strips of pork belly, this will become a firm favourite in your home, too. Try serving on some toasted brioche.

400 g/14 oz. soaked haricot beans (use 200 g/7 oz. dried beans and follow the pack instructions to soak them and keep the liquid to make it up to 400 g/14 oz. in weight)

1 teaspoon mustard powder

2 tablespoons tomato purée/paste

1 tablespoon black treacle/molasses or soft dark brown sugar

1 tablespoon runny honey

1 red onion, finely chopped

1 garlic clove, finely chopped

salt and black pepper, to season

6 chunky pork sausages or 2 strips of boneless pork belly, about 4 cm/2 inches wide (250 g/9 oz. total weight), rind still on

30 x 20-cm/12 x 8-inch roasting pan, greased

SERVES 2

Preheat the oven to 140°C (275°F) Gas 1.

Pour the soaked beans into the greased roasting pan. Mix in the mustard powder, tomato purée/paste, black treacle/molasses, honey, onion, garlic, salt and pepper and pour over the beans.

If you're using pork belly strips, use a sharp knife to score lines in the rind and press salt into the scored lines to help the rind to crackle by dehydrating the fat layer beneath.

Clear little beds in the beans and place the sausages or pork belly strips into the dish.

Cover with foil and bake in the preheated oven for 1½ hours.

Uncover, stir the beans, turn the temperature up to 190°C (375°F) Gas 5 and roast for another 15–20 minutes, until the sausages brown or the pork strips have crackled. (If the beans have dried a little before this happens, just pour in a few tablespoons of water to loosen them.)

To serve, divide the bean mixture between two plates and place the sausages or pork strip on top.

PULLED PORK SHOULDER

This is my very favourite way to have pork shoulder, as it has such a fantastic result when you take a really good-quality piece of pork and slow-cook it to break down the meat. Boneless shoulder pulls really well, but bone-in is even better as you have the bone and the collagen to contribute to the juices and moisture. It's like you're making stock from the inside of your joint to come out through the meat and it produces more juices at the bottom of the pan. If you're cutting your own shoulder, follow the simple way to remove this part (see pages 61–65).

3 kg/6½ lb. free-range, bone-in pork shoulder (rind on, if you would like to make crackling)

1 tablespoon sea salt (flakes or crystals)

3 tablespoons olive oil

1 teaspoon paprika

a big pinch of cayenne pepper

warm brioche rolls, to serve

BARBECUE SAUCE

1 tablespoon olive oil

1 white onion, chopped

1 garlic clove, chopped

2 red (bell) peppers, deseeded and chopped

a pinch of fennel seeds

a pinch of cumin

½ teaspoon mustard powder

½ teaspoon salt

1 tablespoon soft brown sugar

a pinch of black pepper

400 g/14 oz. canned tomatoes, drained

1 cooking apple, cored, peeled and diced

100 ml/generous ⅓ cup cider vinegar

3½ tablespoons maple syrup

100 ml/generous ⅓ cup apple juice

½ teaspoon Dijon mustard

SERVES 10–12

Preheat the oven to 190°C (375°F) Gas 5.

If you want to make crackling, use a sharp knife to score diagonal lines across the rind and push the salt into the cuts in the rind. This draws the moisture out of the rind and fat so that the surface crackles.

Fold a large piece of foil in two to make it double-strength and place it in a roasting pan. You're going to need enough foil either side to cover and seal the pork. Place the pork on top. Drizzle the olive oil over the surface and sprinkle over the paprika and cayenne.

Keeping the foil open at this stage, place the meat in the oven and roast for 25 minutes so that the outside has a chance to brown. Then turn the temperature right down to 150°C (300°F) Gas 2, fold in the sides of the foil so that the meat is totally covered and cook for at least 3 hours, or 4 hours if you can. Every hour, open up the foil and baste the meat by spooning the juices from the bottom of the pan back over the top of the joint. After 3–4 hours, prod it with a fork and see if it is easy to 'pull' (the strips in the muscle should have 'melted' apart). Return for a little longer if it still feels tight.

Open the foil, increase the heat to 200°C (400°F) Gas 6 and continue to cook for 5 minutes to crisp up the top. Remove the crackling and set aside. Use two forks to 'pull' the pork to shreds. Use scissors to cut the crackling into thin strips. Serve the pork in warm brioche rolls with barbecue sauce and crackling on the side.

Barbecue Sauce

Heat the oil in a pan over a medium heat and sauté the onion, garlic and red (bell) pepper for 4–5 minutes, until softened. Stir in the fennel seeds, cumin, mustard powder, salt, sugar and pepper. Add the remaining ingredients and bring to the boil, then turn the heat down to a simmer and cook for 1 hour, stirring occasionally. If it's looking very thick, add a drop more apple juice. Remove from the heat and allow to cool a little, then whizz in a food processor until smooth. Store in a sterilized bottle in the fridge for up to 3 weeks, or freeze in portions to keep for up to 3 months.

SLOW-COOKED LAMB SHANKS

The lamb shank is often thought of as a restaurant cut, but it has become especially popular in recent years. This is partly because it presents really well on the plate and looks very cool. However, it's actually very simple to cook at home. If you're cutting your own leg of lamb, follow the instruction on page 54 to remove the end. I always serve this with Buttery Crushed Potatoes (see page 217).

2 bone-in lamb shanks

20 g/1½ tablespoons butter

2 garlic cloves, roughly chopped

1 lemon, halved

4–6 fresh mint leaves

salt and black pepper, to season

Buttery Crushed Potatoes (see page 217) and Red Onion Gravy (see page 87), to serve

SERVES 2

Pre-heat the oven to 190°C (375°F) Gas 5.

Fold a large piece of foil in two to make it double-strength and place it in a roasting pan. You're going to need enough foil either side to cover and seal the lamb shanks inside.

Rub the butter over all the sides of the meat. Stand the lamb shanks on their flat ends and add the garlic, lemon and mint leaves, and season well.

Keeping the foil open at this stage, place the meat in the oven and roast for 10 minutes, then fold in all the sides of the foil so that the shanks are sealed inside and fully covered. Reduce the oven temperature to 160°C (325°F) Gas 3 and cook for 1 hour.

Remove the foil and prod the meat with a fork. If it feels tender and looks like it's falling off the bone then it's ready. If it still resists the pressure of the fork, you might have a nice chunky-sized shank that will need another 15 minutes or so.

Once it's tender, open up the foil and turn up the temperature again to 190°C (375°F) Gas 5. Pop the lamb shanks back in the oven for 5 minutes to brown and crisp a little.

To serve, spoon the meat juices over the shanks and then put them on serving plates with the buttery crushed potatoes and drizzle more of the meat juices over the top, if you like. Accompany with red onion gravy.

LANCASHIRE HOT POT

This is another example of how some of our traditional recipes, designed for a different time, still perfectly suit our modern meat kitchens. The history of this dish was for the heavily industrialized Northern England to have a recipe that was so easy to throw together in the morning, leave on a low heat in the oven all day, to be devoured after a good day's work. Most of us don't work in jobs that require the physical labour of those times, but we've filled our days and lives with so many other things to keep us just as busy, so to return home to a slow-cooked meal is, in my mind, the very best type of 'ready meal' for a weeknight supper.

6 potatoes

40 g/3 tablespoons butter

100 g/3¾ oz. hard cheese, such as mature/sharp Cheddar (optional)

FILLING

500 g/1 lb. 2 oz. diced mutton or lamb shoulder or loin

2 lamb's kidneys, chopped (optional)

2 white onions, diced

2 carrots, peeled and chopped

½ swede/rutabaga, peeled and chopped

300 ml/1⅓ cups stock

2 tablespoons plain/all-purpose flour

a pinch of dried thyme or a sprig of fresh

1 bay leaf

4 shelled oysters (optional)

salt and black pepper, to season

SERVES 4

Preheat oven to 120°C (250°F) Gas ½.

Start by slicing the potatoes (skins left on) widthways so that they're in oval discs, about 5 mm/¼ inch thick.

Take a large casserole or ovenproof dish (with a lid) and use half the butter to grease it.

Lay half the potatoes across the bottom (this stops the filling catching, too) and up the sides of the pot, if they'll stick.

Throw all the ingredients for the filling into a mixing bowl and mix well. I'm a fan of oysters, but I don't love them in this dish. They were popular at a point but then became expensive so were phased out. It's up to you if you want to add them.

Pour the filling over the potato base and cover the top with the other half of the potatoes, making sure you cover as many of the gaps as possible.

Melt the other half of the butter in a pan or in the microwave and drizzle it over the top of the potatoes. Add a sprinkle more of salt and pepper on the top, then cover with the lid (or with double layer of foil, sealing it very tightly) and bake in the preheated oven for 8–10 hours. For a faster result, preheat the oven to 160°C (325°F) Gas 3 and cook it for 2–3 hours instead.

Just before serving, remove the lid or foil, turn the heat up to 200°C (400°F) Gas 6. If using, grate the cheese onto the top at this stage. Cook for 10 minutes to brown the topping and serve.

JACOB'S LADDER

The short ribs of beef are known as Jacob's Ladder, and the flavour and tenderness of the meat on the bones is delicious. They're great indoors or on the barbecue/ outdoor grill, and they make a very snazzy 'surf 'n' turf' spread with crayfish tails and corn on the cob, as you can pick everything up with your hands and gnaw!

3 garlic cloves, in their skins

4 beef short ribs

3 tablespoons olive oil

4 tablespoons runny honey

3 tablespoons soft brown sugar

400 ml/1²/₃ cups apple cider vinegar

100 g/7 tablespoons butter

salt and black pepper, to season

SURF 'N' TURF

4 crayfish tails or king prawns/ jumbo shrimp

15 g/1 tablespoon butter

a big pinch of chopped fresh parsley

a squeeze of fresh lime juice

4 corn on the cobs, to serve

SERVES 4

Preheat the oven to 180°C (350°F) Gas 4.

Roast the garlic in the oven for 20 minutes with their skins on, then squeeze out the centre. This will give you a sweeter flavour, but if you are short of time, you can just peel and chop the garlic instead.

Cut between the short ribs, through the muscle, and put the separated ribs into a sealable bag or container with a lid. Season with salt and pepper and add the olive oil, honey, 1 tablespoon of the sugar, roasted garlic and apple cider vinegar. Seal the bag or place a lid on the container and set in the fridge for at least 1 hour, but ideally a few hours or overnight.

When you are ready to cook the ribs, preheat the oven to 150°C (300°F) Gas 2.

Take just the ribs out of the marinade and lay them flat in an ovenproof or casserole dish. Cover with a lid or foil and bake in the preheated oven for 2 hours.

Melt the butter in a pan, add the remaining 2 tablespoons of sugar and bring to the boil. Take the ovenproof dish out of the oven and remove the lid. Pour the liquid from around the meat into the pan with the butter and sugar. This has some of the vinegar flavour and a rich stock from cooking the meat on the bone.

Continue cooking the sauce over a high heat until the sauce starts to thicken to a syrupy texture, about 8–9 minutes.

Pour half the sauce back over the ribs, turn the oven up to 200°C (400°F) Gas 6 and return the ribs, uncovered, to the oven for 20 minutes. Turn the ribs over half way through.

Meanwhile, cool the rest of the sauce to thicken it a bit more. Fill a sink with a little very cold water, then lower the bottom of the pan in and stir until it thickens. Pour over the top of the ribs to serve, or serve on the side.

Surf 'n' Turf

To serve this as a classic surf 'n' turf, cook some crayfish tails or king prawns/jumbo shrimp in a pan with some butter until pink and cooked through, then sprinkle with freshly chopped parsley and squeeze with fresh lime. Serve with some corn on the cobs.

OX CHEEK AND BLACKBERRY CASSEROLE

Simply another name for beef cheek, ox cheek is the traditional name in the same way that 'oxtail' is used to describe beef tail. It is too tough to eat if only cooked for a short time. You can imagine how overused the muscle in the cheek is from a lifetime of chewing grass, but also, famously 'chewing the cud', which is the second process of cows' digestion, where the food is chewed all over again! So ox cheek is tough when it's raw and it's a case of the slower the better for cooking it. Like with the Lancashire Hot Pot (see page 168), this could be your 'ready meal' for when you get home from a long day at work.

20 g/1½ tablespoons butter

800 g/1 lb. 12 oz. trimmed, diced ox cheek

2 red onions, chopped

2 tablespoons plain/all-purpose flour

2 carrots, peeled and chopped

2 sticks celery, chopped

400 ml/2⅔ cups Beef Broth (see page 33), or 200 g/7 oz. jellied stock

½ teaspoon all-spice

100 g/3¾ oz. streaky/fatty bacon, diced

1 tablespoon red wine vinegar

2 teaspoons soft dark brown sugar (or 50 g/2 oz. very dark/bittersweet chocolate, minimum 70% cocoa content)

150 g/generous 1 cup blackberries

¾ bottle of red wine

Fancy Mashed Potatoes (see page 217) and green vegetables, to serve

SERVES 4

Preheat the oven to 150°C (300°F) Gas 2.

Melt the butter in a flameproof casserole over a medium heat and brown the diced ox cheek for 1–2 minutes to seal all over.

Add the red onion and fry that for 1 minute. Sprinkle over the flour and don't stir until it changes colour, then add all the other ingredients and give it a good stir.

Put the lid on (or cover with two layers of kitchen foil, sealed tightly) and cook in the preheated oven for 3 hours. If you want to cook it all day, preheat the oven to 120°C (250°F) Gas ½ and cook it for 8 hours instead.

To thicken the sauce a little before serving, move the casserole back to the stovetop and stir it over a very high heat for a few minutes until it thickens – don't worry, the cheek won't toughen again, they are already very tender.

This dish is dark and rich but still lovely and sweet. I like to serve it with mash and some green vegetables.

Want to make it even easier? Don't worry about browning the cheek first. It adds a little extra roasty flavour but there is still so much flavour and richness, you can just chuck all the ingredients in the casserole, mix it around, and pop it in the oven.

BEEF CASSEROLE WITH HERBY DUMPLINGS

This casserole couldn't be easier, as you just throw it all in a pan and leave it to cook in the oven. The herby dumplings are optional, but they make a lovely addition if you like the sound of them. Serve with some fresh green vegetables. This is a perfect winter warmer to divide into portions and freeze. You can freeze the dumplings separately too, if you want to make extra for other dishes.

20 g/1½ tablespoons butter

1 red onion, chopped

60 g/1 cup chopped mushrooms

1 red (bell) pepper, deseeded and chopped

400 g/14 oz. diced beef (cut from the rib joint, see page 45)

75 ml/6 tablespoons red wine

90 ml/7 tablespoons Brown Chicken Stock (see page 32) or ½ chicken stock/bouillon cube

1½ tablespoons plain/ all-purpose flour

1 bay leaf

a pinch each of salt and black pepper

green vegetables, to serve

HERBY DUMPLINGS

70 g/¾ cup beef suet or vegetable shortening

150 g/generous 1 cup plain or all-purpose flour

a pinch of dried rosemary

a pinch of dried thyme

SERVES 4

Preheat the oven to 160°C (325°F) Gas 3.

Put all of the casserole ingredients into a pan over a medium heat and bring to the boil with a lid on, stirring a few times to make sure nothing catches on the bottom and the flour breaks up.

Once boiling, keep the lid on and transfer to the preheated oven. Cook for 1 hour, giving it a stir after 30 minutes. (Meanwhile, see below to make the herby dumplings, if you want to add them.) If the casserole isn't quick thick enough after an hour of cooking, return it to the oven for a further 15 minutes.

Serve with some green vegetables and the herby dumplings.

Herby Dumplings
Mix the suet, flour and herbs in a bowl. Add 1–2 tablespoons of water, a little at a time, until you can squeeze the mixture into a solid ball. Pinch off a piece at a time – a sphere to fit in the circle you make when you join your index finger and thumb is a good size. Roll them tightly and place on a baking sheet. After the casserole has been in for 30 minutes, put the baking sheet in the oven and bake the dumplings for 15 minutes. Then throw them into the casserole for the last 15 minutes of the casserole's cooking time.

STEAK AND KIDNEY PIE

This is another age-old meat dish that still works fantastically well in our modern meat kitchens. It's also a good one for entertaining because it can be prepared earlier in the day or the day before and then simply put in the oven when ready.

20 g/1½ tablespoons butter, plus extra if needed

750 g/1 lb. 10 oz. diced beef (cut from the rib joint, see page 45)

250 g/9 oz. beef or lamb's kidneys, diced

2 white onions, chopped

3 carrots, peeled and chopped

60 g/1 cup mushrooms, chopped

1½ tablespoons plain/all-purpose flour

a pinch of freshly chopped thyme leaves

a pinch of freshly chopped sage

4 teaspoons tomato purée/paste

2 teaspoons Worcestershire sauce

800 ml/3⅓ cups Beef Broth (see page 33)

salt and pepper, to season

PASTRY

200 g/1½ cups plain/all-purpose flour, plus extra for dusting

100 g/7 tablespoons butter, at room temperature

a pinch of freshly chopped tarragon (optional)

a pinch of salt

1–2 tablespoons cold water

1 beaten egg, to glaze

20-cm/8-inch round pie dish, greased with butter

SERVES 4

Melt the butter in a frying pan/skillet over a medium heat and set a large pan on another burner over a medium heat.

Brown the diced beef first in the frying/pan, in batches, and add it to the pan as soon as is it sealed. Do the same with the diced kidneys – you don't need to cook these through, it's just browning for flavour at this stage.

Add the onion, carrots and mushrooms to the frying pan/skillet, adding a little more butter if necessary, and soften them for a few minutes, letting them loosen any meaty bits from the bottom of the frying pan/skillet. Pour the vegetables into the pan and give it a stir, then sprinkle the flour over the top. Don't stir again until the flour starts to change colour. Stir in the thyme, sage, tomato purée/paste and Worcestershire Sauce and season with salt and pepper. Pour in the beef broth and bring to the boil, then reduce the heat to a low simmer and leave for up to 2 hours, with the lid half-on.

It might be thick enough after 90 minutes, so just keep giving it a stir occasionally and making sure none of the flour has caught on the bottom. Add a little more beef broth if it's too thick. If it isn't thickening, remove the lid completely and increase the heat a little.

Preheat the oven to 180°C (350°F) Gas 4.

Make the pastry by rubbing the flour and butter together with your fingertips until it resembles breadcrumbs. Add the salt and the cold water, a tablespoon at a time, until the pastry holds together.

Lightly dust a work surface with flour. Use a rolling pin to roll out the dough to a size sufficient to generously cover your pie dish. Use your finger to run butter around 2 cm/¾ inch of the outside edge of the pie dish. If you have a pie funnel, put this in the centre of the dish. (This enables the steam to escape, keeping the pastry crisp.)

Pour the filling mixture into the pie dish. Lift up the pastry and place it on the top of the filling. Use a sharp knife to cut a small cross in the centre of the pastry lid (directly on top of the pie funnel, if using). Trim the edges or let them overhang, as preferred, and press around the edge to seal it to the sides of the pie.

Using a pastry brush, glaze the top of the pie with the beaten egg. Transfer the dish to a baking sheet to catch any escaping filling and bake in the preheated oven for 30–40 minutes, until the top is golden brown and crisp. Serve with peas and a glass of amber ale.

VENISON AND CHORIZO CASSOULET

A cassoulet is a slow-cooked casserole and it is actually often the easiest and least fiddly approach to a casserole, so it suits our modern meat kitchens perfectly.

a 400-g/14-oz. piece of venison loin, diced

100 g/3¾ oz. chorizo, diced

20 g/1½ tablespoons butter

50 g/scant 1 cup sliced mushrooms

1 red (bell) pepper, deseeded and diced

1 red onion, diced

1 garlic clove, chopped

150 ml/⅔ cup red wine

2 tablespoons plain/all-purpose flour

200 g/1¼ cups dried haricot/navy beans, soaked and drained or 250 g/1¾ cups pre-soaked canned haricot/navy beans, drained

a pinch of fresh or dried tarragon

2 teaspoons redcurrant jelly

300 ml/1¼ cups White Chicken Stock (see page 32)

salt and pepper, to season

SERVES 2

Preheat the oven to 150°C (300°F) Gas 2

Put all of the ingredients into a casserole with a lid, give it a good stir and put the lid on. Put it in the preheated oven and cook for 2½–3 hours. That's it!

It'll keep chilled for a week in the fridge or it freezes really well if you make a larger batch and freeze it in portions. Just increase the cooking time by 15 minutes per extra serving, if you are increasing the quantities.

ROASTS

CLASSIC ROAST CHICKEN

If you've been good enough to read the introduction to this book, you'll know how much value I place on the life of the animal. There is no better visual aid for demonstrating the difference between good farming and cheap farming than a roast chicken. Start with a well-farmed, free-range chicken and, whatever your ethics, you will be rewarded with a succulent, flavoursome, easy-to-carve roast, which doesn't disappear to half its original size.

20 g/1½ tablespoons butter, softened

1 whole chicken, approx. 2 kg/4 lbs., trimmed and prepared

1 lemon

1 garlic clove, sliced lengthways

2 sprigs of fresh thyme

salt and black pepper, to season

Easy Roast Gravy (see page 200) and your choice of accompaniments, to serve

SERVES 6

Preheat the oven to 180°C (350°F) Gas 4.

Rub the butter over the whole chicken, being careful not to break the skin.

Wash and roughly zest half of the lemon, and rub the zest into the skin. Rub the cut sides of the garlic halves over the skin too. Set the garlic aside; do not discard it.

Lay the chicken in a roasting pan, breast down to start with, so you start with the flat side (its back) facing up.

Cut the lemon in half and squeeze the juice of half the lemon over the top of the chicken. Don't throw the squeezed lemon half away – add it to the roasting pan. Sprinkle a big pinch of salt and black pepper over the top.

Put the other half of the lemon inside the chicken, along with the sprigs of thyme and reserved pieces of garlic.

Roast the chicken in the preheated oven for 45 minutes. After this time, turn it over in the dish so it is breast-side up. Sprinkle salt and black pepper on the top and return to the oven for another 45 minutes.

Press a fork into the thickest part of the leg. If the juices are still pink, it needs to be cooked for longer – return to the oven for another 10 minutes and check again.

Serve with gravy and your choice of veg.

Leftovers
Any leftover roast chicken can be whipped into a delicious chicken noodle soup the next evening (see page 185).

LEFTOVER ROAST CHICKEN NOODLE SOUP

A lovely leftover idea for Classic Roast Chicken (page 182) or Roast Turkey (page 212), and so easy to throw together for a light and nutritious weeknight supper.

1 tablespoon olive oil

1 red chilli/chile, deseeded and chopped

1 garlic clove, finely chopped

1 tablespoon Thai fish sauce

1 teaspoon tamarind paste

1 teaspoon soft brown sugar

1 teaspoon turmeric

a pinch of cumin

a pinch of ground ginger (or 1.5 cm/¾ inch root ginger, finely chopped)

4 spring onions/scallions, chopped (and/or other stir-fry vegetables as you like)

150 ml/⅔ cup coconut milk

about 300 g/10½ oz. leftover roast chicken (or however much you have), shredded

700 ml/scant 3 cups White or Brown Chicken Stock (see page 32)

100–200 g/3¾–7 oz. dried noodles, depending on how hungry you are

salt and black pepper

fresh coriander/cilantro leaves, to serve

a sprinkle of sesame seeds, to serve (optional)

SERVES 2

Heat the oil in a pan with tall sides that is large enough to hold a litre/quart of liquid over a medium heat. Fry the chilli/chile and garlic with the fish sauce, tamarind paste, sugar, turmeric, cumin, ginger and a good pinch each of salt and pepper.

Add the spring onions/scallions and cook until golden. Pour in the coconut milk, add the shredded leftover chicken and cook until the mixture starts to bubble. Pour in the stock and bring back to the boil. Bubble the soup for 4–5 minutes.

Follow the packet instructions to cook your noodles, but most need only a few minutes cooking time, so add them into the soup and cook for the required amount of time.

Serve with a sprinkle of fresh coriander/cilantro on top. To add a bit of toasty crunch, heat a dry frying pan/skillet over a medium heat and toast a handful of sesame seeds for 1–2 minutes until brown. Sprinkle them on the top, too.

STUFFED ROLLED PORK SHOULDER

This is a fantastic Sunday roast and it looks very impressive despite its relatively low cost. The shoulder/butt is an inexpensive cut, but it contains lots of fat under the skin which makes for a moist and flavourful piece of meat.

1.2–1.4 kg/2¾–3 lbs. boneless pork shoulder/butt, ideally unrolled with skin still on

Easy Roast Gravy (see page 200), roast potatoes, honey parsnips and green beans, to serve

STUFFING

30 g/¼ stick butter

a pinch of salt

1 red onion, finely diced

1 garlic clove, finely diced

300 g/10½ oz. chicken livers

1 cooking apple, finely diced

a pinch of freshly chopped parsley

a pinch of freshly chopped or dried sage

100 ml/scant ½ cup red wine

a pinch of black pepper

butcher's twine, about 60 cm/2 feet in length

SERVES 4

Start with the stuffing. Heat a pan with the butter and salt over a high heat and then sauté the onion, garlic, chicken livers and cooking apple for 4–5 minutes until softened.

Reduce the heat a little and add the parsley, sage and pepper, and stir well. Add the red wine and bring to the boil for 2–3 minutes to thicken.

Remove from the heat and allow to cool – to speed up the cooling process, fill a sink with cold water, submerge the base of the pan in the cold water and stir until the mixture has cooled. Alternatively, make the stuffing mix earlier in the day and move to the fridge once it's at room temperature.

Preheat the oven to 180°C (350°F) Gas 4.

Lay the pork flat on a board, skin-side up. Take a very sharp knife and score lines across the skin of the pork. You do not want to cut all the way through to the meat; just score through the surface of the skin.

Turn the pork over. Take the cooled stuffing mixture and rub it into the underside of the shoulder, across the pink pork meat. Really push it into the gaps and corners so it's spread across the whole side.

Roll the shoulder/butt and secure it using butcher's twine (see page 26 for instructions on how to tie). Now push salt into the scored gaps in the skin; this will help draw out the moisture in the rind to produce crackling.

Transfer the rolled meat to a roasting pan, with the skin facing up, and roast in the middle of the oven for 80 minutes. Use a meat thermometer to check the inside of the joint (see charts on page 29) and insert a skewer into the meat to check if the meat juices are running clear. Roast for longer if necessary, until cooked through.

Cut lovely, big, thick slices to serve with easy roast gravy, roast potatoes, honey parsnips and green beans.

CLASSIC ROAST LEG OF LAMB

A rich and juicy roast lamb is often such a popular option, and you can't go too wrong with the cooking of it either, because the shape and ratio of meat to bone makes it the perfect cut for a well-balanced roasting. If you're cutting your own lamb leg, follow the preparation instructions on pages 53–55. I like the classic combination of mint sauce with roast lamb, so I've included an easy recipe here.

bone-in, trimmed leg of lamb (usually around 2 kg/4 lbs.)

2 sprigs of fresh rosemary

2 garlic cloves, chopped (optional)

salt and black pepper, to season

Easy Roast Gravy (see page 200) and your choice of accompaniments, to serve

MINT SAUCE

10–12 fresh mint leaves, chopped finely

2 tablespoons soft brown sugar

2 tablespoons boiling water

2 tablespoons white wine vinegar

SERVES 6–8

Preheat the oven to 180°C (350°F).

Place the leg of lamb in a roasting pan and sprinkle the rosemary, garlic (if using), and some salt and pepper on top.

If you like, put your vegetables to roast around the edge (I recommend parboiling for a couple minutes first, if you're doing potatoes or root vegetables, so that they don't dry out too much).

Cook in the preheated oven for about 90 minutes, but check it a couple of times before the end of that time, as cooking times depend on the shape of the leg – they can be short and plump or long and thin, depending on the breed. For rare/pink meat, it may only need 60 minutes.

I find the easiest way to carve is to start in the middle and slice towards the ankle end first. Then you can hold that and turn it to slice in the opposite direction. There's lots of meat on the hind leg, so don't worry too much about technique; you'll be able to get all the meat off one way or another.

Serve with the mint sauce (see below), easy roast gravy and vegetables of your choice. If you have any leftover, why not use it in the leftover roast lamb moussaka (see page 191).

Mint Sauce

Put the chopped mint leaves and brown sugar in a cold frying pan/ skillet and pour over the boiling water (or just enough to soak up and dissolve the sugar).

Put the pan over a high heat and bring to the boil. Add the white wine vinegar and boil for another couple of minutes.

Leave to cool; ideally cool it to room temperature then let it chill in the fridge overnight. Alternatively, submerge the bottom of the pan in a sink of cold water and stir so that the mint sauce cools and thickens a bit. Serve cold with the roast lamb.

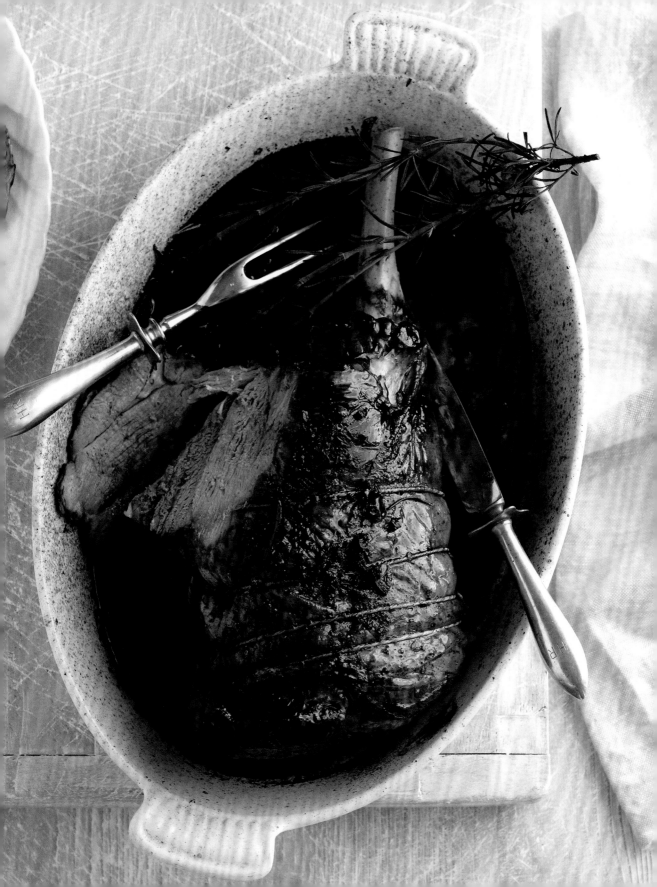

LEFTOVER ROAST LAMB MOUSSAKA

You can use the leftovers from Classic Roast Leg of Lamb (see page 188) or the Lamb Kleftiko with Spiced Yogurt (see page 146) for this simple and delicious Greek-inspired recipe. It is a perfect comforting Monday-night dinner to use up the remnants of your Sunday roast. Serve it simply with some crisp salad.

2 potatoes

olive oil, for drizzling and frying

salt and black pepper,
to season

1 aubergine/eggplant

1 white onion, diced

1 garlic clove, finely chopped

a pinch of fresh or dried
oregano

a pinch of ground nutmeg

a pinch of cinnamon

2 tablespoons plain/all-purpose
flour

150 ml/⅔ cup white wine

120 ml/½ cup full-fat/whole
milk

freshly squeezed juice of
½ lemon

300–400 g/10½–14 oz. leftover
roast lamb (from the Lamb
Kleftiko or Classic Roast Leg
of Lamb on pages 146 and 188)

200 g/7 oz. drained canned
chopped tomatoes

salad, to serve

SERVES 2

Preheat the oven to 180°C (350°F) Gas 4.

Slice the potatoes widthways, 5-mm/¼-inch thick to make oval discs (leave the skins on). Layer the potato discs flat on a greased baking sheet and drizzle olive oil on the top. Season with a good pinch of salt and black pepper. Bake in the preheated oven for 20 minutes until they start to brown.

Meanwhile, slice the aubergine/eggplant widthways, into similar sized discs. Heat a little olive oil in a frying pan/skillet and fry the aubergine/eggplant discs in batches in one layer, until soft and starting to brown, and then remove and lay on paper towels to absorb some of the excess oil.

In the same pan, fry the onion and garlic over a medium heat until soft and brown. Mix in a pinch of salt and pepper, and the oregano, nutmeg and cinnamon. Add the flour and stir to make a paste, then add the white wine. Stir until smooth and then slowly add the milk, a little at a time, to make a smooth sauce. Stir in the drained chopped tomatoes.

Pour half the mixture from the frying pan/skillet into a greased roasting pan. Tear or cut the leftover lamb pieces into bite-sized strips or pieces and layer half of the lamb on top of the mixture in the roasting pan.

Then layer half the potato discs followed by half the aubergine/eggplant on top.

Repeat with the remaining ingredients, following the same order, finishing with the potatoes on top.

Cover with foil and bake in the preheated oven for 15 minutes. Remove the foil and place under a hot grill/broiler for 5–10 minutes until the potatoes have crisped on top. Serve with a crisp salad.

ROAST RACK OF LAMB

For a modern meat kitchen, this is a great recipe for a really quick roast. The little cutlets have all the flavour and tenderness of a slow-cooked leg roast, but they take just 25 minutes to cook to perfection.

1 top end rack of lamb, French trimmed/Frenched (about 6–7 ribs)

4 garlic cloves, roughly chopped

salt and black pepper, to season

6–7 tablespoons olive oil

2–3 Maris Piper or Yukon Gold potatoes, peeled, quartered and parboiled

2 carrots, peeled and cut into large chunks

1 red onion, chopped into large chunks

a handful of cherry tomatoes

SERVES 2

Preheat the oven to 190°C (375°F) Gas 5.

Lay the rack bone-side down. Score the top and put the garlic pieces in some of the lines. Sprinkle salt and pepper on the top and drizzle over 3 tablespoons of the olive oil.

Place the parboiled potatoes, carrots, red onion and cherry tomatoes in a roasting pan. Drizzle over the remaining olive oil and sprinkle with some salt and black pepper.

Put this in the oven for 20 minutes, then give it all a good shake and place the lamb on top. Return to the oven for 25–30 minutes (25 minutes will keep the lamb a little pink inside).

Remove the lamb from the pan and allow to rest for a few minutes, before slicing between the bones to make cutlets. Serve with the roast vegetables.

WHISKY LAMB SHOULDER

The marinade for this makes the absolute most of the lamb flavours. As the lamb falls apart in your mouth, I hope you'll also have the same experience of the sweetness first, then the lovely lamb and herb combinations, and then a bold finale of the whisky taste.

4 teaspoons vegetable oil

2 tablespoons runny honey

5 tablespoons whisky (I used a single malt Scotch whisky)

a big pinch of fresh rosemary

a splash of apple cider vinegar

bone-in shoulder of lamb (around 1.5 kg/3 lbs.)

salt and black pepper, to season

your choice of vegetables, to serve

SERVES 4

Mix the vegetable oil, honey, whisky, rosemary, cider vinegar and some salt and pepper in a large mixing bowl. Add the lamb and coat it in the marinade.

If you have a large, sealable food bag, move the meat and all the marinade to the bag and seal with as little air inside as possible. Place in the fridge to marinate for at least 2 hours, ideally overnight.

Preheat the oven to 160°C (325°F) Gas 3.

Remove the lamb shoulder from the bag, reserving the marinade. Place it on a large piece of foil. Pour all the marinade over the top and fold up the sides of the foil to scrunch and seal over the top of the meat. Place in a roasting pan.

Place in the preheated oven and roast for at least 2½ hours, but ideally 3 hours for really tender meat.

To serve, lift the meat out of the foil, but make sure you reserve the juices to pour onto the lamb once you have carved it. (If you plan to make the leftover whisky lamb shoulder wrap on page 196 the next day, it's a good idea to set aside some of the juices in a jug/pitcher. Slice only what you will need for now, and keep the rest of the lamb on the bone, as this will keep it nice and moist until the next day.)

Serve with accompanying vegetables of your choice.

LEFTOVER WHISKY LAMB SHOULDER WRAP

This is an easy supper or lunch to enjoy the day after you make the Whisky Lamb Shoulder (see page 195), especially nice on a warm evening in the summer. This will fill 2 large tortilla wraps or 4 smaller ones. Place all the filling ingredients on the table for both diners to fill their own wraps.

1 aubergine/eggplant

2 tablespoons olive oil

2–4 flour tortilla wraps

2–4 tablespoons natural/plain yogurt

2–4 teaspoons redcurrant jelly

2–4 handfuls of baby leaf spinach

100 g/3¾ oz. feta cheese (optional)

300–400 g/10½–14 oz. leftover roast lamb (from Whisky Lamb Shoulder, see page 195), torn into pieces

SERVES 2

Slice the aubergine/eggplant into 5 mm/¼ in. thick slices.

Heat the olive oil in a ridged griddle/grill pan or frying pan/skillet over a high heat, then fry the aubergine/eggplant slices, in batches if necessary. Once cooked, transfer them to paper towels to soak up some of the excess oil. Leave the pan over the heat.

Wet the tortilla wraps slightly on both sides to help them crisp, then add them to the pan you have just cooked the aubergine/eggplant in, heating them one at a time. Cook them on one side (to keep the other side grease-free) until warmed and slightly crispy. Alternatively, heat them according to the packet instructions.

To serve, place a tortilla wrap (greasy-side up) on a plate and spread the yogurt and redcurrant jelly down the middle.

Lay the shredded lamb on top and sprinkle the spinach and feta cheese, if using, on top.

Fold the end and sides over the middle to make a wrap.

ROAST RIB OF BEEF

I think this is the most impressive-looking cut of beef and, with a bit of prep, it can deliver the most incredible beef experience – my favourite. I recommend planning for about 400 g/14 oz. per person of raw beef rib, which will yield about 250 g/ 9 oz. of meat each, or work it out as 1 rib bone per 2–3 people.

For step-by-step techniques and advice on preparing your rib of beef for roasting, see pages 45–47.

three-bone rib of beef (about 3 kg/6 lbs.)

salt and black pepper, to season

Yorkshire Puddings (see page 201), Foolproof Roasties (see page 200), Easy Roast Gravy (see page 200) and your choice of vegetables, to serve

SERVES 6–8

Preheat the oven to 190°C (375°F) Gas 5.

Put your prepared rib of beef in a roasting pan and sprinkle a good pinch of salt over the top cap of fat as well as a little black pepper.

Roast in the preheated oven for 20 minutes and then reduce the heat to 160°C (325°F) Gas 3 and roast for a further 2 hours (or 20 minutes per 500 g/1 lb.) for medium.

Turn off the oven, open the door to let the heat out and then shut the door again, leaving the beef to sit in the warm oven, still uncovered, for 15 minutes. (This is not ideal if you're roasting vegetables at the same time, so you can remove the meat and leave it to stand in as warm a place as possible if you are cooking vegetables in the oven.)

Remove the twine and place the meat on a carving board. Don't throw away any of the juices – you can use them to prepare the gravy. Serve the meat with yorkshire puddings, foolproof roasties, easy roast gravy and your choice of vegetables.

ACCOMPANIMENTS

EASY ROAST GRAVY

One of the many joys of a good roast dinner is that it's really easy to make a gravy at the end, in the few minutes while the meat is resting.

2 tablespoons plain/all-purpose flour
100 g/3¾ oz. Brown Chicken Stock (see page 32) or 200 ml/scant 1 cup chicken stock from a stock/bouillon cube
2 teaspoons redcurrant or cranberry jelly
salt and black pepper, to season

SERVES 6

Once your meat is fully roasted, move it to a board to rest (don't put kitchen foil over the top; you'll only be a few minutes, so just let it breathe).

Drain nearly all of the meat juices from the roasting pan into a jar, but leave the last 3–4 tablespoons in there – this is usually the fattier portion, which is what we want.

Put the roasting pan over a medium heat on the stovetop and let the reserved fatty meat juices start to bubble.

Stir in the flour and then add the stock and stir well until smooth. Add the redcurrant or cranberry jelly and keep cooking until thickened and glossy. Season to taste.

Transfer to a gravy boat or spoon over the carved meat.

FOOLPROOF ROASTIES

We put a lot of pressure on ourselves to make the perfect roasties. Here's a simple recipe for the way that always works best for me.

6 Maris Piper or Yukon Gold potatoes, peeled and quartered
100 g/3¾ oz. goose fat or 100 g/7 tablespoons butter
1 tablespoon plain/all-purpose flour
salt, for the water

SERVES 4

Preheat the oven to 200°C (400°F) Gas 6 and put a roasting pan in the oven to heat up.

Put the potatoes in a pan of water with a pinch of salt. Bring to the boil then reduce the heat to low and simmer for 2 minutes.

Meanwhile, remove the hot roasting pan from the oven and put the goose fat or butter in. Return it to the oven to get really hot.

Drain the potatoes well in a colander. Take the lid from the pan and hold it securely over the top of the colander, then shake, shake, shake for 15 seconds to roughen the edges a little. Sprinkle with the flour.

Carefully put the potatoes into the hot fat (be wary of splashing) and roast in the preheated oven for 15 minutes. Turn all the potatoes over and return to the oven for a further 15 minutes. If they're still not quite crispy, turn them again and replace for a further 10 minutes, until golden brown and crispy.

YORKSHIRE PUDDINGS

Made from a basic batter of eggs, flour and milk, these classic British puddings remain a traditional part of a Sunday roast, however modern our tastebuds become!

3 eggs, beaten

200 g/1½ cups plain/all-purpose flour, sifted

250 ml/1 cup full-fat/whole milk

salt and black pepper, to season

an 8–10-hole muffin pan, greased well with butter or dripping

MAKES 8–10

Preheat the oven to 180°C (350°F) Gas 4.

Beat the eggs into the sifted flour, then use a whisk or electric hand-held whisk to mix while you add the milk. Mix until smooth and season with salt and pepper.

Place the batter in the fridge for 30 minutes to rest.

To help the batter brown well on the underside and ensure a good rise, put the greased muffin pan in the preheated oven for the last 5 minutes of the batter's resting time.

Take the hot pan out of the oven and divide the batter between the holes. Put it back in the oven and cook for 25–30 minutes, but keep checking the puddings after 20 minutes and remove once risen and golden brown.

HONEY PARSNIPS

This is an easy-peasy accompaniment that's scrummy with a roast dinner and heavenly for leftovers. You could also give carrots the same treatment, or try swapping the honey for maple syrup.

2 tablespoons olive oil

4–5 parsnips (depending on how chunky they are), peeled and quartered

4 tablespoons runny honey

1 teaspoon mustard powder (optional)

salt, for the water

SERVES 4

Preheat the oven to 180°C (350°F) Gas 4.

Put the olive oil in a roasting pan and place in the oven to heat up.

Bring a pan of water to the boil over a high heat, add the quartered parsnips and a pinch of salt and boil for 2 minutes. Drain well.

Take the hot roasting pan out of the oven and tip the parboiled parsnips into the hot oil carefully, being wary of spitting oil. Toss the parsnips in the hot oil to coat them all over.

Roast the parsnips for 5 minutes in the preheated oven to dry them out a little. Then drizzle the honey over the top, sprinkle with salt and return to the oven for 15–20 minutes, until sticky and brown. You can also add mustard power along with the honey, if you like.

LEFTOVER ROAST BEEF SANDWICH

This is the ultimate leftovers lunch and one of my favourite sandwiches. It is perfect for using up leftovers from the Roast Rib of Beef (see page 199) or the Flash Fillet Roast (see page 153). Use whatever bread you prefer for your sandwich – sliced, bagel, roll or anything you fancy.

2 slices of bread, or a bagel or roll of your choice

1 garlic clove, skin still on

2 rashers/strips streaky/fatty bacon (optional)

20 g/1 oz. Stilton or other blue cheese, thinly sliced

2–3 slices of leftover roast beef

1–2 cherry tomatoes, as ripe as possible, sliced

SERVES 1

Preheat the oven to 200°C (400°F) Gas 6.

Put the garlic clove (skin still on) on a baking sheet and cook in the preheated oven for 10 minutes.

Fry the bacon in a frying pan/skillet over a medium heat until crisp and cooked to your liking. Set aside on paper towels to soak up any excess oil.

Meanwhile, lightly toast the bread, bagel or roll.

Set the roasted garlic aside to cool, then once it's cool enough to handle, squeeze out the inside of the garlic clove by cutting off the hard end and gently squeezing the soft centre.

Butter the bread, bagel or roll and then spread the soft garlic purée on top. Place the Stilton or blue cheese slices on top, then add your leftover roast beef, followed by the tomato slices and finally the crispy bacon.

If you are taking this to work, wrap it in brown paper and secure it with twine, then try to pretend you don't notice the envy of all your work colleagues when you get it out at lunch time.

ROAST GOOSE

Roast goose makes a pleasant alternative to roast turkey at Christmas or for a special Sunday roast. It has a very different flavour to turkey, but a similar approach is taken for roasting it and for keeping it as succulent as possible. A goose is much more about the breasts than turkey or chicken – in fact, you don't get an awful lot off the thighs and drumsticks. There is something really special about the dark, rich taste of roasted goose breast though, a delight. See page 214 for the Roast Turkey Stuffing and Turkey Giblet Gravy. As a guide, I suggest 500 g/1 lb. per person to yield about 200 g/7 oz. boneless meat.

a whole goose, about 4.5 kg/ 9 lbs.

100 g/7 tablespoons butter

1 quantity Roast Turkey Stuffing (see page 214, optional)

salt and black pepper, to season

about 200 ml/scant 1 cup chicken stock or any other type of stock that you have

a handful of fresh sage and parsley

SERVES 8–10

Preheat the oven to 160°C (325°F) Gas 3.

Use tweezers to remove any stubborn feathers left in the skin of the goose. Rub the butter over the skin of the bird. Fill with the stuffing, if using.

Sprinkle salt and black pepper all over the bird and place the goose breast-side down on a rack inside a roasting pan.

Pour in the stock up to a depth of 2 cm/¾ inch, along with the fresh sage and parsley.

Roast in the preheated oven for 20 minutes, then turn the goose over and spoon the juices over the top (the breasts).

Return to the oven for a further 20 minutes per 1 kg/2 lbs. of unstuffed goose weight.

Baste every 20 minutes to keep it succulent.

Increase the heat to 200°C (400°F) Gas 6 for the last 15 minutes to brown the surface and crisp the skin without drying out the meat.

LEFTOVER ROAST GOOSE, MANGO AND AVOCADO SALAD

The richness of goose makes it a terrific meat for salads. It works well in wraps and rolls, but it turns a salad into a hearty, flavoursome meal and there are lovely dressing options to go with it too. This is an excellent recipe idea for using up the leftovers from the Roast Goose (see page 205). However it also works well with duck breasts; you'll need 1 duck breast per person.

about 400 g/14 oz. leftover Roast Goose (see page 205), or 2 duck breasts

2 handfuls of salad leaves

2 spring onions/scallions, trimmed and finely sliced lengthways

1 avocado, stoned/pitted, peeled and sliced

1 mango, ripe as possible, stoned, peeled and sliced

8–10 baby plum tomatoes, halved

DRESSING

2 tablespoons soy sauce

freshly squeezed juice of 1 lime

1 teaspoon ground ginger

2 tablespoons sesame oil

a big pinch of chilli powder

salt and black pepper, to season

SERVES 2

If you are using leftover roast goose, tear the meat into shreds and set it aside. If you are roasting duck breasts for this salad, preheat the oven to 180°C (350°F) Gas 4. Score the skin of the duck breasts and season with salt and pepper. Heat a little olive oil in an ovenproof frying pan/skillet and cook the duck breasts over a high heat, skin-side down, for a few minutes until the fat starts to crisp. Turn the duck breasts over and transfer to the preheated oven. Roast the duck breasts in the preheated oven for 15–20 minutes, or until cooked to your liking.

Mix all the dressing ingredients together and season to taste.

Divide the salad leaves and spring onions/scallions between two serving plates and toss them with half the dressing.

Layer the avocado, mango, tomatoes and goose or duck on top, and drizzle over a little extra dressing.

HONEY AND MUSTARD HAM HOCKS

Lovely served as a roast with accompaniments or cold for picnics or sandwiches, this is a classic flavour combination for ham and works perfectly with the juiciness of meat from a well-used cut like the hock

1 large or 2 small ham hocks, smoked or unsmoked

1 carrot, trimmed and roughly chopped (unpeeled)

1 white onion, roughly chopped

1 celery stick, roughly chopped

2 garlic cloves, roughly chopped

a sprig of fresh tarragon

3 teaspoons wholegrain mustard

1 teaspoon English mustard powder

4 tablespoons clear honey

2 teaspoons soft brown sugar

salt and black pepper (or pink peppercorns if you have them), to season

SERVES 4

Cut the rind off the ham hock(s) and discard. Put the ham hock(s) in a large pan or pot. Add the carrot, onion, celery, garlic and enough water to cover and bring to the boil over a high heat. Reduce the heat to low and leave to simmer for 1 hour 30 minutes.

Preheat the oven to 180°C (350°F) Gas 4.

In a bowl mix the tarragon, mustards, honey, sugar and a pinch of salt and pepper (or pink peppercorns, if using).

Remove the ham hock(s) from the pan or pot, place in a roasting pan and cover with the honey and mustard glaze. Roast in the middle of the preheated oven for 1 hour, but turn and baste it (or them) every 10–15 minutes by using a spoon to scoop up the liquid from the bottom of the pan and drizzle it back over the top.

GLAZED ROAST GAMMON

I've tried this marinade on a few types of gammon/ham – smoked, unsmoked, sweet-cured – and it seems to work well with all of them. My favourite with these flavours is an unsmoked (sometimes called 'green') shoulder (or 'horseshoe') gammon/ham. Allow about 200 g/7 oz. per person or serving... and plan for lots of cold leftovers! This is best when marinated for a few hours or overnight.

1–1.2 kg/2–2 lbs. 7 oz. gammon joint/boned ham

bread and butter and piccalilli or other pickle, to serve (optional)

CRANBERRY GLAZE

20 g/1½ tablespoons butter

1 red onion, finely chopped

2 handfuls of fresh cranberries (frozen cranberries, defrosted, work well here)

a big pinch of ground cinnamon

2 tablespoons white wine vinegar

1 tablespoon soft dark brown sugar

freshly squeezed juice of ½ lemon

SERVES 4

Start by making the glaze. Heat the butter in a frying pan/skillet over a medium heat and fry the red onion for about 4–5 minutes until soft and brown.

Add the cranberries and cinnamon, fry for 1 minute and then pour in the white wine vinegar. When the vinegar comes to the boil, sprinkle in the sugar and stir well.

Add the lemon juice, stir again and remove from the heat. Leave to cool until it is cool enough to touch (you don't want the heat of the glaze to cook the meat at all).

Lay out a piece of foil that is large enough to fold around the gammon/ham fully. Score lines all over the gammon/ham and spread the glaze all over it. Push the glaze mixture into the scored lines with your fingers to really push the flavour into the meat.

Move the gammon/ham to the foil and wrap it tightly, then put it in the fridge for a minimum of 3 hours or overnight, ideally.

Preheat the oven to 190°C (375°F) Gas 5.

Put the gammon/ham, still in the foil, onto a baking sheet. Open out the top of the foil, then put in the preheated oven. Roast for 10 minutes, then reduce the heat to 170°C (340°F) Gas 4. Baste the meat by spooning the mixture at the bottom of the foil over the top of the meat and return to the oven for 20 minutes.

Baste again and return to the oven for another 40 minutes.

If you want to crisp up the top any more, just turn the heat back up to 190°C (375°F) Gas 5 for the last 5 minutes of cooking.

Allow to rest for 6–8 minutes, then carve and serve warm or leave to cool completely and serve cold with piccalilli or other pickle of your choice.

ROAST TURKEY

This recipe is for Thanksgiving, Christmas or any gathering requiring something bigger than a chicken! I've learned (via plenty of trial and error!) that turkey is the best thing to prove that 'good meat' is easier to cook than cheaper alternatives. On top of that, there are a couple of things you can do to help keep it really juicy.

a whole turkey, about 4.5 kg/ 9 lbs.

100 g/7 tablespoons butter, softened

salt and black pepper, to season

about 1 kg/2 lb. Roast Turkey Stuffing (see page 214, optional)

Turkey Giblet Gravy (see page 214), Foolproof Roasties (see page 200), Honey Parsnips (see page 201) and any other vegetables of your choice, to serve

PIGS IN BLANKETS

16–20 chipolatas

8–10 rashers/strips streaky/ fatty bacon

SERVES 8–10

Preheat the oven to 190°C (375°F) Gas 5.

Use tweezers to remove any stubborn feathers left in the skin of the turkey. Place the bird on a rack, breast-side down, and then place the rack into a roasting pan.

Take the butter and rub it all over the skin of the bird, making sure you get it into the folds of the legs too. Sprinkle salt and black pepper all over the bird. Fill with the stuffing, if using.

Pour 2 cm/³⁄₄ inch of water into the base of the roasting pan, underneath the rack.

Roast on the bottom shelf of the preheated oven for 45 minutes, then turn the bird over and baste by using a spoon to scoop the liquid from the bottom of the pan over the bird. Sprinkle over a little more salt and black pepper.

Return to the oven for 1 hour more, but remove the bird and baste it every 15 minutes. After this time, check to see if it's cooked: at the thickest part of the leg, scratch the surface with a fork and press down. If the juices are still pink, return to the oven for another 10 minutes and check again. If your turkey is bigger or smaller than the one used here, you can work out the total cooking time at 25 minutes per 1 kg/2 lbs. unstuffed weight.

Follow the instructions on page 230 to make turkey giblet gravy while your turkey is roasting, if you like.

Allow the turkey to rest for 8–10 minutes. Serve with the gravy, stuffing, roast potatoes, parsnips, pigs in blankets and any other accompaniments you choose.

Pigs in Blankets

Preheat the oven to 180°C (350°F). Cut each slice of bacon in half and wrap each half-slice around a chipolata. Roast in the preheated oven for 15–20 minutes, until the bacon is crisp and the sausages are cooked through.

ROAST TURKEY STUFFING

Cooking time for your turkey or goose needs to be calculated for the unstuffed bird, so make sure you weigh it before stuffing. This recipe also works really well for stuffed goose too – I just replace the chestnuts with 2 peeled, cored and chopped cooking apples. I have also included a recipe for making delicious gravy using the giblets from your bird. Perfect for Christmas or Thanksgiving.

20 g/1½ tablespoons butter

1 white onion

a big pinch of fresh sage

a big pinch of freshly chopped parsley

a handful of dried apricots

50 g/½ cup beef suet or vegetable shortening

80 g/1 cup dried breadcrumbs

1 beaten egg

150 g/5 oz. cooked chestnuts

1 lemon, halved

200 g/7 oz. minced/ground pork

salt and black pepper, to season

TURKEY GIBLET GRAVY

giblets from the turkey

1 carrot, roughly chopped

1 celery stick, roughly chopped

1 white onion, roughly chopped

60 ml/¼ cup red wine

2 tablespoons plain/all-purpose flour

salt and black pepper, to season

a pinch of freshly chopped tarragon or parsley and a squeeze of lemon juice (optional)

SERVES 8–10

Put the butter, onion, sage, parsley, apricots, suet or shortening, breadcrumbs, beaten egg and chestnuts into a food processor. Squeeze in the lemon juice from both halves, but keep one of the squeezed halves for later. Whizz until finely chopped.

Transfer the stuffing mixture to a mixing bowl and add the ground/minced pork. Mix together and season well. Stuff into the cavity of the bird and used the reserved lemon half to partly seal the entrance.

Turkey Giblet Gravy

While your turkey is roasting, put the giblets in a pan, add the chopped carrot, celery and onion. Cover with water and bring to the boil. I like to remove the liver from the giblets as it's a stronger flavour than I prefer in my gravy, but feel free to use it if you like. Reduce the heat to a low simmer and cook for as long as it takes to roast the turkey.

Once your turkey is cooked, take the bird and the rack out of the roasting pan and place the roasting pan (if it is flameproof) over a low heat on the stove top to keep it bubbling.

Be sure to scrape off any crispy bits from the edge of the dish to get all the flavour into the gravy. Add 150 ml/⅔ cup of the giblet stock and the red wine, and mix well.

Sprinkle in the flour, let it colour and then stir well until the gravy starts to thicken. Taste and add salt and pepper. Tarragon is also lovely in a gravy for turkey or a pinch of parsley and a squeeze of lemon juice, if you want to lighten it.

ROAST DINNER SAUCES

BREAD SAUCE

500 ml/2 cups full-fat/whole milk

50 g/3½ tablespoons butter

2 shallots, chopped

1 teaspoon cloves

1 teaspoon black peppercorns

2 garlic cloves, chopped

1 bay leaf

a sprig of fresh thyme

a big pinch of ground or freshly grated nutmeg

100 g/scant 2 cups fresh white breadcrumbs

3 tablespoons double/heavy cream

salt, to taste

SERVES 4–6

Put all the ingredients except the breadcrumbs and cream in a pan and bring to the boil.

Reduce the heat to low and simmer for 25 minutes.

Remove from the heat and strain to capture just the liquid.

Return to the heat and add the breadcrumbs, then keep stirring until it starts to thicken. Add the double/heavy cream and stir well. Add salt to taste.

Serve warm straight away or make it up to 3 days before you need it and store it chilled in the fridge.

APPLE SAUCE

10 g/2 teaspoons butter

5–6 cooking apples, peeled, cored and diced

finely grated zest of ½ lemon

freshly squeezed juice of 1 lemon

a pinch of ground cinnamon

1 tablespoon soft light brown sugar

100 ml/scant ½ cup water

salt, to taste

SERVES 4–6

Melt the butter in a pan over a medium heat. Add all the other ingredients and bring to the boil, then reduce the heat to a low simmer and leave for 20–30 minutes until thick and the apples are soft, stirring occasionally to make sure it's not catching on the base of the pan. Add salt to taste.

Either mash it with a potato masher or purée it in a food processor, or just dish it up chunky, depending on your preference.

Store in the fridge for up to 2 weeks in a sealed container.

CRANBERRY SAUCE

20 g/1½ tablespoons butter

1 red onion, finely chopped

2 handfuls of fresh cranberries (frozen cranberries, defrosted, work well here)

a big pinch of cinnamon

2 tablespoons white wine vinegar

1 tablespoon soft dark brown sugar

freshly squeezed juice of ½ lemon

SERVES 4–6

In a frying pan/skillet, heat the butter over a medium heat and fry the onion until soft and golden brown.

Add the cranberries and cinnamon, then fry for 1 minute. Pour in the white wine vinegar and bring to the boil, then sprinkle in the sugar and keep mixing well.

Add the lemon juice, stir and remove from the heat.

Serve immediately while hot or chill and serve as a cold accompaniment.

Store in the fridge for up to 2 weeks in a sealed container.

PERFECT POTATOES

TRIPLE-COOKED CHIPS

3–4 potatoes, depending on size
vegetable oil, for deep-frying

SERVES 2

Wash the potatoes and remove any blemishes. Keep the skins on and slice into chunky chips/fries.

Bring a pan of water to the boil, add the chips/fries and boil for 8 minutes to soften.

Drain in a colander, then use the lid of the pan to cover and shake for a few seconds – not as hard as for roast potatoes, as you don't want the chips/fries to break.

Heat the oil for deep-frying in a large pan until it bubbles – use a tester chip/fry first to make sure it sizzles as you put it in.

Tip the chips/fries in and fry for 8 minutes, then use a slotted spoon to fish them out and drain on paper towels to cool.

Preheat the oven to 200°C (400°F) Gas 6.

Transfer the chips/fries to a baking sheet, making sure they are in one layer and not touching each other.

Cook in the preheated oven for 8 minutes, or until as crispy as you like. Serve immediately.

DAUPHINOISE POTATOES

400 ml/scant 1¾ cups double/heavy cream
400 ml/scant 1¾ cups full-fat/whole milk
4 garlic cloves, roughly chopped
a little freshly grated nutmeg, to taste
a sprig of fresh thyme
salt and black pepper, to season
4–5 potatoes, peeled
150 g/1⅓ cups grated Gruyère cheese (or mature/sharp Cheddar cheese)

a 20-cm/8-inch square baking dish, greased

SERVES 4

Preheat the oven to 180°C (350°F) Gas 4.

Put the cream, milk, garlic, nutmeg and thyme into a pan, add a pinch of salt and pepper, and bring to the boil.

Slice the potatoes widthways into oval discs, about 3 mm/⅛ inch thick.

Add the potato slices to the simmering cream mixture and cook for 10 minutes.

Use a slotted spoon to scoop out the slices of potato and lay them into the prepared dish. Discard the thyme.

Pour the rest of the liquid over the top until it's just about to cover the top layer of potatoes.

Sprinkle the grated cheese on top.

Bake in the preheated oven for 30 minutes until browned on top and the liquid is absorbed. If they're still not browning, you can cook them under a hot grill/broiler for 5 minutes.

FANCY MASHED POTATOES

3–4 potatoes, peeled and quartered
20 g/1½ tablespoons butter
40 g/½ cup finely grated Parmesan cheese (optional)
2 tablespoons double/heavy cream
salt and black pepper, to season

SERVES 4

Bring a pan of salted water to the boil, add the potatoes and cook for 25 minutes until totally soft when you prod them with a fork.

Drain and return to the pan. Add the butter and mash until lovely and soft.

Mix in the Parmesan, if using, and then the double/heavy cream, salt and pepper.

Serve immediately or use within in 2 days (keep sealed in the fridge and make sure you cool it fully before moving it to the fridge so that it doesn't sweat).

BUTTERY CRUSHED POTATOES

8–10 new potatoes
20 g/1½ tablespoons butter
salt and black pepper, to season

SERVES 2

Heat a grill/broiler to medium.

Boil the new potatoes (skins on) in a pan of salted boiling water for 20 minutes, until soft.

Drain and return to the pan.

Add the butter and swirl to melt.

Tip the buttery potatoes onto the greased baking sheet and crush with a fork.

Sprinkle salt and pepper on the top and pop under the preheated grill/broiler for 5 minutes to brown.

BOXING DAY PIE

The ultimate celebration of leftovers! Boxing Day is a bank holiday celebrated on 26 December in the UK. This is my mother's recipe and she realized, even from when my sister and I were very young, that we were asking for tiny portions of the separate meats and vegetables on Christmas Day because we were trying to stockpile as much as possible for her Boxing Day pie! If you're out and about for the few days after Christmas, this is also a brilliant way to trim and freeze all the leftovers for another time. It just takes 15 minutes without cooking, so you can sort out the whole fridge in a single recipe.

about 1.5 kg/3 lbs. Christmas or Thanksgiving leftovers, such as turkey or goose, ham, bacon, sausages, stuffing, sprouts, roast potatoes, carrots, parsnips, bread sauce or peas

WHITE WINE SAUCE

50 g/3½ tablespoons butter

1 teaspoon mustard powder

50 g/6 tablespoons plain/all-purpose flour, sifted

700 ml/scant 3 cups full-fat/whole milk

150 ml/⅔ cup white wine

salt and pepper, to season

TOPPING

100 g/scant 2 cups fresh breadcrumbs

100 g/1⅓ cup finely grated Parmesan cheese or grated Cheddar cheese

SERVES 4

Preheat the oven to 180°C (350°F) Gas 4.

To make the sauce, melt the butter in a pan over a medium heat and sprinkle in the mustard powder and flour.

Add a pinch of salt and pepper and then slowly add the milk, a little at a time, mixing well with the butter and flour base.

Once all the milk is added, keep stirring continuously over the heat until the sauce begins to thicken. Once it is the consistency of double/heavy cream, add the wine and reduce to a low simmer.

Taste and add more seasoning as you like.

Then take all the leftovers and slice everything you can into strips and discs. My mother even slices the roast potatoes and sprouts, and there are always lovely big chunks of the ham shredded in there too. Any leftover sausages are sliced lengthways to make thin strips.

Layer them all in a large roasting pan, however you like. We tend to be a bit particular and have separate layers of each, but you can honestly just throw it all in. Pour the white wine sauce over the top.

Mix the breadcrumbs and Parmesan or Cheddar together in a bowl and sprinkle over the top.

Bake in the preheated oven with foil on top for 20 minutes, then remove the foil for another 20 minutes. If you want to brown the top a little more to serve, just pop it under a preheated grill/broiler for a few minutes until crispy and browned.

I like to serve this with lots of ketchup on the side, but it's also nice with leftover cranberry sauce.

SOURCES

UK
INGREDIENTS

**BLYTHBURGH REAL
FREE RANGE PORK**
St Margaret's Farm
Mells, Halesworth
Suffolk, IP19 9DD
+44 (0)1986 873 298
www.freerangepork.co.uk

FOREST PIG CHARCUTERIE
Bell Farm, Far Forest
Kidderminster
Worcestershire, DY14 9DX
+44 (0)1299 266 771
www.forestpig.com

ISLE OF MAN MEATS
Meat Plant,
Ballafletcher Farm Road
Tromode, Douglas
Isle of Man, IM4 4QE
+44 (0)1624 674 346
www.iommeats.com

J. F. EDWARDS
42 Central Markets
West Market Building
London, EC1A 9PS
www.jfedwards.uk.com

LITTLE GATE FARM
Horseshoe Lane, Beckley
East Sussex, TN31 6RZ
+44 (0)1797 260 580
www.littlegate.org.uk

OCADO
Ocado Limited
Freepost 13498
PO BOX 3 62
Hatfield, AL9 7BR
+44 (0)345 656 1234
www.ocado.com

PACKINGTON FREE RANGE
Blakenhall Park
Barton-under-Needwood
Staffordshire, DE13 8AJ
+44 (0)1283 711 547
www.packingtonfreerange.
co.uk

**TREALY FARM
CHARCUTERIE**
Park Farm, Plough Rd
Goytre, Abergavenny
Wales, NP4 0AL
+44 (0)1495 785 090
www.trealyfarm.com

WAITROSE
Customer Service
Waitrose Ltd.
Doncastle Road, Bracknell
Berkshire, RG12 8YA
+44 (0)1344 825 232
www.waitrose.co.uk

EQUIPMENT

BUTCHERS' SUNDRIES
TruNet House
Ivanhoe Business Park
Ashby-De-La-Zouch
Leicestershire LE65 2UZ
+44 (0)1530 411 275
www.butchers-sundries.com

**NISBETS CATERING
SUPPLIES**
Nisbets Plc., Fourth Way
Avonmouth
Bristol, BS11 8TB
+44 (0)117 316 5000
www.nisbets.co.uk

JOHN LEWIS
www.johnlewis.com

LAKELAND
Alexandra Buildings
Windermere
Cumbria, LA23 1BQ
+44 (0)1539 488 100
www.lakeland.co.uk

PROCOOK®
Davy Way
Waterwells
Gloucester GL2 2BY
+44 (0)330 100 1010
www.procook.co.uk

DIVERTIMENTI
227–229 Brompton Road
London, SW3 2EP
+44 (0)207 581 8065
www.divertimenti.co.uk

US
INGREDIENTS

BROKEN ARROW RANCH
3296 Junction Highway
Ingram, TX 78025
+1 (800) 962-4263
www.brokenarrowranch.com

FATTED CALF
644 C First Street
Napa, CA 94559
+1 (707) 256-3684
and 320 Fell Street
San Francisco, CA
+1 (415) 400-5614
www.fattedcalf.com

HERITAGE FOODS U. S. A.
790 Washington Ave.
PMB 303
Brooklyn, NY 11238
+1 (718) 389 0985
www.heritagefoodsusa.com

MAINE MEAT
7 Wallingford Square #104
Kittery, ME 03904
+1 (207) 703 0219
www.memeat.com

PARADISE LOCKER MEATS
405 W. Birch St.
Trimble, MO 64492
+1 (816) 370-MEAT
www.paradisemeats.com

REVIVAL MARKET
550 Heights Boulevard
Houston, TX 77007
+1 (713) 880-8463
www.revivalmarket.com

THE BUTCHER & LARDER
Chicago, IL
+1 (773) 687-8280
www.thebutcherandlarder.
com

THE SPOTTED TROTTER
Atlanta, GA
www.thespottedtrotter.com
+1 (404) 254-4958

TAILS & TROTTERS
Portland, OR
www.tailsandtrottersco.com
+1 (503) 477-8682

EQUIPMENT

BUTCHER PACKER
www.butcher-packer.com
+1 (248) 583-1250

EMILIO MITI
www.emiliomiti.com

**NATURAL CASING
COMPANY**
www.naturalcasingco.com
+1 (715) 582-3736

THE SAUSAGE MAKER
www.sausagemaker.com
+1 (716) 824-5814

INDEX

ACKNOWLEDGMENTS

Julia, Kate, Leslie, Cindy, Maria, Mel and all the team at Ryland, Peters & Small, who put such incredible effort into getting any book commissioned, edited, produced, printed, listed, distributed... It is a total pleasure working for you and I'm immensely grateful for the opportunities.

Steve Painter, the calm, skilled, amazing photographer, prop stylist and designer, I loved working with you in Hastings. Thank you for all your work. And Lucy McKelvie the gorgeous daffodil – thank you for your wonderful food styling. Alex and Hilary McNeill and their chickens, and Claire and Dave Cordell and everyone at Little Gate Farm who let us shoot on location.

Georgina, Sean, Sam, Beth and Bev, our founding shop crew, and all the current Muddy Boots team for freeing up my time to get to have a go at this book and for being on this crazy journey with us.

Francesca, Lauren and the team at Prestbury for letting me camp out in their offices to focus on writing the introduction. Nick, Sandy and Mike for welcomed breaks from the typing. And these three with Jon for making up our ambitious little Muddy Boots family.

The farms, abattoirs, producers and inspiring food companies my husband Roland and I get to work with. Thank you for the incredible supply and all the hard work you do.

My father-in-law, John – the inspiration behind all the respect I have for land and farming. We saw you still be exhilarated by the birth of every calf and your honorable sadness when they left fully grown. Thank you for letting us live at your farm and learn about what you do.

Sarah, Dan, Linda, Dunc, Alex, Amelia, Totty, Harry, Freddie – I completely adore you, Ballards!

My brother-in-law, Paddy, and two incredible girls, Orla and Nuala. And my big sister, Olivia... I still just basically want to be you.

My bonkers parents, Edward and Jude. You crack me up. I have too much to thank you for.

And Ro... I still haven't found the words. I'll find them, I promise.